THE ⊦

Ciara

1

THE HOLY SPIRIT

© 2016, 2019 by Ciaran J. Thompson

Bible quotations are taken from:

the 21st Century King James Version®, copyright © 1994. Used by permission of Deuel Enterprises, Inc., Gary, SD 57237. All rights reserved.

the Amplified® Bible (AMP), Copyright © 2015 by The Lockman Foundation Used by permission. www.Lockman.org" ESVUK,

the British English HOLY BIBLE, NEW INTERNATIONAL VERSION® NIV®. Copyright © 1973, 1978, 1984, 2011,

the Holy Bible, New Living Translation, copyright ©1996, 2004, 2007, 2013, 2015 by Tyndale House Foundation. Used by permission of Tyndale House Publishers, Inc., Carol Stream, Illinois 60188. All rights reserved,

the New King James Version®. Copyright © 1982 by Thomas Nelson.

Words underlined or added in brackets in Bible quotations are added for emphasis to help clarify the point that is being made.

~

Published through Amazon.
Third Edition

Edited by Julie Miller and Mary Rose Sims.

The original paperback version was published on the second anniversary of Ray Granner's passing in August 2017, to whom this book is in part dedicated to.

The front and back covers are designed to convey the water and fire of the Spirit as described in this book and in the Holy Bible.

~

*This is dedicated to a dear friend, mentor and the most Spirit-led,
Christ-like person I have ever known - Paul Miller (1949-2015).
His spirit and humility inspired me to complete this work.*

*Your impact and legacy still lives on Paul
in the countless numbers you influenced.*

~

*This is also dedicated to Ray Granner (1929-2015), who was so
passionate for God, the Gospel and the need to be filled with the
Holy Spirit. The prayer group he began and one where he gave
me opportunities to use my gifts is now celebrating more than 21
years of ministry.*

*Your passionate love for the Lord still inspires,
Ray.*

~

~

With grateful thanks to Franci Ball,
who for as long as I've known her
has always believed in me,
and whose wisdom helped me
create the very first foundations of this book.

~

THE HOLY
SPIRIT

Ciaran J. Thompson

May this book bless you in Jesus' great name

C. Thompson

CONTENTS

FOREWORD

Paul Miller's dear wife, Julie has not only helped to edit this book, but has also kindly and graciously written the foreword. Her wisdom in the whole process has greatly aided me in better handling the Word of truth and understanding the Spirit of truth:

Together with my late husband, Paul, I have known Ciaran for many years – Paul dished out teaching and wisdom and I dished out tea and biscuits! Over that time, we had witnessed an emerging teaching ministry through his love of the scriptures and his desire for truth in order to further God's Kingdom in our lives and that of the world in which we live.

This book is a workable, comprehensive guide to the third person of the Holy Trinity - the Holy Spirit. It is the Holy Spirit who draws us closer to Jesus and the Father through His work in our hearts - who brings us comfort, joy, wisdom, with whom we can speak and who can guide us through difficult times in our lives.

It is the Holy Spirit who makes all the difference between believing in God and letting Him live through us to bring healing and peace, not only in our lives but also to a world filled with fear, wars, abusive relationships, addictions, sorrow, aimlessness etc. A world where so many are in need.

This book will bring understanding and deal with the issue of 'how to' know Jesus through the Holy Spirit, hear Him speak to us, know God's heart in our hearts. We pray... 'Thy Kingdom Come', but this will not happen without us opening our hearts to His Holy Spirit, letting Him see through our eyes, hear through our ears, speak through our mouths, having His love and compassion flowing through our spirits to a broken and fallen world.

As in the words of a well-known hymn....

> *Thank you Oh My Father*
> *for giving us your Son*
> *And leaving your Spirit*
> *till the work on earth is done.*

(Green, 1982)

Julie ended with those famous words from 'There is a Redeemer', showing the complimentary work of the Father, Son and Spirit. It is my desire that this book will be the first of three on the Trinity. The orthodox way to write three books on the Trinity would be to begin with the Father, however I want to turn our understanding of the Godhead on its head, by beginning with the Holy Spirit.

I believe, He is the least understood person of the Godhead and the one we need a fresh revelation on here and now. He is the one who has been left on the Earth until "the work is done" and He is the Spirit of Christ who leads us back to the Father. So, if we begin with Him, we will grow our understanding and faith in who God is.

INTRODUCTION

The Holy Spirit is very important. As one reads through the Bible, it is clear that the Holy Spirit plays a central role from start to finish - appearing in its first and last chapters. The New Testament is clear that His power should be seen in the lives of all believers in Christ.

In accordance with common Biblical Christian teaching, it is also clear that the Holy Spirit is divine. Being often referred to as the third member of the Godhead. The belief being that there is God the Father, God the Son and God the Spirit - and yet only one God.

This is a challenge to understand and explain. I do not believe anyone will ever fully comprehend the nature of God. If they could, God wouldn't be God. God is bigger and greater and more mysterious than any human being could understand or explain and yet we can have a relationship with Him as Father, Son and Spirit. Through Church history, many Christians have argued about the Godhead and indeed, the Spirit of God, leading to many ignoring or even dismissing the Holy Spirit altogether.

Back in the fourth century, there was a major disagreement over a single phrase in a church statement of faith concerning the role of the Holy Spirit. This greatly deepened the splits already forming between the Western and the Eastern Churches at the time. But rather than being quiet and passé about the Spirit of God, (who by my count is mentioned at least 300 times in the Bible) I

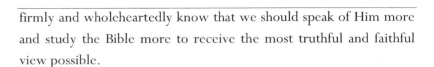

firmly and wholeheartedly know that we should speak of Him more and study the Bible more to receive the most truthful and faithful view possible.

The Bible includes many words encouraging Christians to be led by the Spirit of God and even to be filled by His presence in their very souls. After all, He played a major role in the formation of the once unified church, which is now split in so many ways.

As a result of the many splits that now exist, there have been an increasing number of leaders and members from across church denominations calling for reunification of the church body. Calls for closer links to be forged were steadily gathering pace around the time of the 500th anniversary of the perhaps the greatest split in Church history - the Reformation of 1517.

I believe that there needs to be more love, cooperation and unity amongst the faithful in line with Christ's own call for His followers to **"be one"** (John 17:21). Even so, I am nevertheless deeply concerned that we are going to see a growing degree of 'false unity' - which is warned about in scripture (Matt. 24:36, 2 Tim. 4:3-4). A unity whereby many churches will try to heal past wounds by compromising the truth of God's Word and by actually attempting to repent of positive steps made to retain truth and hold back deception.

After all, the Word of God is a two-edged sword that divides as well as unifies. It separates what is shallow from what is deep (see: 2 Chr. 30:12, Matt. 10:34-36, Eph. 2:14-22, Heb. 4:11-12). I believe, we have to decide if we are going to be shallow and weak or deep and faithful to the truth before God and before the world.

Within the context of His prayer for unity as quoted above, Jesus also said that His followers needed to be sanctified by **"the Word [which] is truth"** and by **"the Spirit of truth"** (see: John 16-17). Indeed, the word, 'sanctify' means 'to make holy'. Only the purifying effect of the 'Holy' Bible and the work of the 'Holy' Spirit can all believers find a Godly, truthful unity together again. Paul Miller often said that we should not have unity at any cost, and as I say, it must be bought at the price of truth.

From the Bible, here are some firm words to the Ephesian church leaders:

> <u>Keep watch over yourselves and all the flock of which the Holy Spirit has made you overseers</u>. Be shepherds of the church <u>of God</u>, which he bought with his own blood. I know that after I leave, savage wolves will come in among you and will not spare the flock. Even from your own number men will arise and <u>distort the truth in order to draw away disciples after them</u>. <u>So be on your guard!</u> Remember that for three years <u>I never stopped warning each of you</u> night and day with tears. Now I commit you to God and to <u>the word</u> of his grace, which can <u>build you up</u> and give you an inheritance <u>among all those who are sanctified</u>.

> (Acts 20:28-33, see also: Prov. 29:18, 1 Cor. 15:33).

I believe the key to retaining the fundamental truths of God's Word and at the same time encourage much-needed love, trust and unity amongst believers is to wholeheartedly ask God to lead us by His Spirit in truthfully discerning His will and by rightly interpreting and applying His Word (see: 1 Pet. 1:22).

This *must* come from a genuine place, for God sees our hearts anyway. We cannot deceive Him. The Word of God "judges the thoughts and attitudes of the heart. Nothing in all creation is hidden from God's sight. Everything is uncovered and laid bare before the eyes of him to whom we must give account." (Hebrews 4:12-13). After all, we do not want to be a 'savage wolf', but rather, an 'innocent sheep' who follows the Good Shepherd (see also: Matt. 7:14-20, John 10:1-18).

If we do all the above, I believe that we will be able to see through lying spirits of deception, which the Bible says would increasingly try to sow division in the age of the church:

Now the Spirit expressly says that in later times some will depart from the faith by devoting themselves to deceitful spirits and teachings of demons, through the insincerity of liars whose consciences are seared, who forbid marriage and require abstinence from foods that God created to be received with thanksgiving by those who believe and know the truth. For everything created by God is good, and nothing is to be rejected if it is received with thanksgiving, for it is made holy by the word of God and prayer...[do] not to quarrel about words, which does no good, but only ruins the hearers.

Do your best to present yourself to God as one
approved, a worker who has no need to be ashamed,
rightly handling the word of truth.

1 Timothy 4:1-5; 2:14-15

What we should aim for is this:

> ...with all humility and gentleness, with patience, [let
> us bear] with one another in love, eager to maintain the
> unity of the Spirit in the bond of peace. There is one
> body and one Spirit - just as you were called to the one
> hope that belongs to your call - one Lord, one faith,
> one baptism, one God and Father of all, who is over all
> and through all and in all.
>
> Ephesians 4:2-6

Notice how Paul proclaims truths there alongside a call to
peace and unity. I understand that it is difficult at times to achieve
this with other believers. It is often easier to argue over differing
interpretations than to agree on the fundamentals. I myself have had
my fair share of arguments and debates with fellow Christians over
the years!

Anyway, returning to the main topic of the Holy Spirit - I
believe that He is the unseen divine presence of God, who can be
felt at times. The Bible describes Him coming in the form of a dove,
a fire, a breath, a wind, and that tangible manifest presence (see: 1
Kings 8:10-11, Psalm 51:11; 139:7, Luke 3:21-22, John 20:22,
Acts 2:1-6; 4:31). Therefore, it can be more difficult to relate to

Him and even to explain His very existence than it is concerning Christ - who became a man. Similarly, the Spirit is more difficult to understand and explain than the Father - as we all have had the experience of knowing our own earthly father or at least a father-figure. Many of us are fathers as well.

The basic reality of parenthood can help us understand about the Father and we can relate to Christ's humanity by studying His life, but the unseen, unhuman Holy Spirit is more difficult to comprehend. Maybe that is in fact evidence of His existence - He is beyond our full comprehension and actually *has* to be in order to be who the Bible says He is. Perhaps only those who have experienced His undeniable presence and power truly know He is real.

Indeed, Jesus Himself commanded His earliest followers to receive the Holy Spirit, because He would not be with them in human form forever, but would be with them in spirit (John 14-16; 20:22).

We discover this by reading the Bible. So, in order to know the Spirit of God more, we must know the Word of God more. In fact, the Bible itself claims to be inspired by the Holy Spirit (see: 2 Tim. 3:16-17). There is an inextricable link between the Spirit and the Word. One explains the other.

This leads me to the reason why I wrote my own book on the matter. It is my hope that it will encourage people in their knowledge and love of God the Holy Spirit. I have seen His work in my life - strengthening and helping me and making me more like Christ. I want as many people as possible to experience this for themselves!

This book is not a massive in-depth, theological exegesis of the matter, nor is it entirely devotional in nature. It falls somewhere in the middle, and hopefully at a level that all people can appreciate. It is important to emulate Christ our Saviour as best we can. For He spoke simply, yet profoundly. It is indeed His Spirit living within us that provides us with the ability to be more like Him (John 14:26, Rom. 8).

But before we move forward, I want to put a little disclaimer out there. Though many refer to the Holy Spirit in neutral terms by using 'it' or with feminine terms such as 'She' and 'Her', I will stick to using the masculine 'He' and 'His'. This is done for several reasons:

- the Bible refers to God as 'Father' and uses male pronouns to describe Him (Jer. 3:19, Psa. 2:12, Rom. 15:13)

- Jesus Himself came as a man and described both the Father and the Spirit with masculine pronouns (John 16:7-17, Phil. 2:8).

- the Book of Acts describes how "**he** had not fallen" on one group of believers and also of how "**he** [spoke] through Isaiah"

- in Romans, Paul says, "The Spirit **himself** testifies with our spirit…" (see: Acts 8:16; 28:25-27, Romans 8:16-17).

Though I do not believe the Spirit *has* a gender, I think it makes more sense to maintain the same identification as with the Son and the Father, especially when looking at the original Greek words used. I do not see this as a sexist matter, it is just the way God chose to reveal Himself, His Son and His Spirit. Indeed, God made both male and female in His image and endowed them with equal value (Gen. 1:27, Gal. 3:28).

1.

THE PERSON + ROLE OF THE SPIRIT

"The Spirit gives life;
the flesh counts for nothing.
The words I have spoken to you
- they are full of the Spirit and life. "

John 6:63

The name for the study of the Holy Spirit is called 'Pneumatology'. This is so named as 'pneúma' is the Greek word for 'spirit'. The word 'pneúma' is used throughout the original Greek New Testament and can also refer to a breath or a gust of wind. As for the Old Testament (which was mostly written in Hebrew), we find the word, 'ruakh' being used for 'spirit', 'breath' and 'wind'.

This wonderful word first appears as early as the second verse of the entire Bible (Genesis 1:2), where we read of the Spirit of God hovering of the Earth as it was being made ready for life to appear. We next read of the Spirit in the following chapter. Here, God breathes life into the first man, making him "a living soul" (Genesis 2:7).

Those two verses establish the main role of the Holy Spirit as seen throughout the Bible - to give both physical and spiritual life to all the peoples God had made (see: Psa. 104:29-30 and Gal. 6:8).

Some of you reading this will be more familiar with the title 'the Holy Ghost', as many older English translations of the Bible (i.e. the King James Version) use the Old English word 'gast'. It effectively means the same as 'spirit'.

Throughout the Bible, we read about the work of the Holy Spirit at many different times and in many different ways. He also has many different titles, roles and attributes as well:

- In Genesis and Job, He is called 'the Breath of God', who is involved in the creation process, and throughout the Old Testament He is usually called 'the Spirit', 'the Spirit of God' and 'the Spirit of the Lord', with just three mentions of Him as 'the Holy Spirit'.

- The writers of the New Testament adopted all those titles, but preferred towards the use of 'the Holy Spirit'. This maybe in order to emphasise the indwelling of God's holiness within each believer. A privilege only granted to believers from Pentecost onwards (see: Acts 2:16-17). (See: 'Pentecost and the fulfilment of prophecy' in Chapter 6 for more on this).

- Jesus called the Spirit 'the Advocate', 'the Counsellor', 'the Helper', 'the Comforter', 'the Spirit of the Father' and as with John the Apostle in his first letter, He called Him 'the Spirit of truth'.

- The apostolic writers Paul and Peter collectively called Him 'the Spirit of Jesus', 'the Spirit of Christ', 'the Spirit of Jesus Christ' and Peter also called Him 'the Spirit of glory'.

- The Book of Hebrews titled Him the 'the Spirit of grace' and in Revelation, John described Him as 'the Seven-fold Spirit' who went out from Heaven into all the world.

Using those titles, roles and attributes, here is a breakdown of the approximate number of references to the Holy Spirit in the Bible:

THE SCRIPTURES	MENTIONS OF THE HOLY SPIRIT
The Old Testament	45
The books of law	10
The books of history	20
The books of poetry	10
The books of prophecy	5
The New Testament	255
The gospels	65
The book of Acts	55
The epistles and letters	115
The book of Revelation	20

With roughly 300 mentions, it is clear that the Holy Spirit should be a key figure to all believers in God. Even in stories of the Bible where the Holy Spirit is not specifically mentioned, His work is clearly seen in many of the lives of those involved. When people in the Bible were inspired or felt God's presence or heard His voice - it was His Spirit at work in their spirit (see: Num. 11:25, 2 Sam. 23:2, Ezek. 2:2, Rom 8:16, 26-27).

The Spirit of God is credited with inspiring all the writings and prophecies of the Old Testament (OT).

Peter states that:

...no prophecy of <u>Scripture</u> comes from someone's own interpretation. For no prophecy was ever produced by the will of man, but men spoke from God as they were <u>carried along by the Holy Spirit</u>.

2 Peter 1:20-21

Paul states that:

All <u>Scripture is breathed out by God</u> and profitable for teaching, for reproof, for correction, and for training in righteousness, that the man of God may be competent, equipped for every good work.

2 Timothy 3:16-17

What of the New Testament? Well in order for the above two passages to apply, the New Testament (NT) must be considered "Scripture" as well. To that end, consider these points:

- In 1 Corinthians 15:3-7, Paul says that that "Christ died for our <u>sins according to the Scriptures</u>, that he was buried, that he was raised on the third day <u>according to the Scriptures</u>". It is quite likely that Paul is referring to the Gospels (or at least to one of them) - as they are the only books of the Bible that recorded Christ's death, burial and resurrection in detail. I believe Paul is citing a detailed written account of Christ - probably Mark's writings, seen as he and Mark were friends, and Mark's Gospel and 1 Corinthians were written around the same time - in the AD 50's.

- In 1 Timothy 5:18, Paul quotes Deuteronomy 25:4 and Luke 10:7 together and calls them both "Scripture", therefore putting NT writings on the same level as the OT.

- In 2 Peter 2:19, Peter refers to this saying, "people are slaves to whatever has mastered them." He could be quoting from the Book of Romans, where it says "...when you offer yourselves to someone as obedient slaves, you are slaves of the one you obey..." (see: 6:16). As prominent Bible commentator, Charles Ellicott (1819–1905) puts it, "There is nothing improbable in St. Peter being well acquainted with the Epistle to the Romans during the last years of his life; the improbability would rather be in supposing that he did not know it." (Ellicott, 1897).

- In 2 Peter 3:15-16, Peter does indeed refer to the writings of Paul and puts them on the same level as "the other Scriptures". The wider context of those words also show that Peter regarded his own letters alongside that of Paul's. Therefore, the above statements from Peter and Paul about the Spirit's role in inspiring the OT writings can surely apply to at least Peter and Paul's writings as well.

- The second last book of the Bible - Jude alludes and even quotes 2 Peter several times and puts them alongside references to the Old Testament. He clearly saw Peter's words as authoritative enough to use as a foundation for his message.

- In addition to all that, Jesus told His disciples (many of whom went onto write the books of the NT) that:

...the Holy Spirit...will teach you all things and bring to your remembrance <u>all</u> that I have said to you...the Spirit will receive from me what <u>he will make known to you</u>.

John 14:26; 16:15

As established above, the Old Testament writers were clearly inspired by the Spirit in what they wrote. Their writings are called 'Scripture'. The guiding theme of their writings concerns the coming of a Saviour, who would one day liberate God's people from their sins. As we know, that person was Jesus Christ, and it is the New Testament writers who describe for us His fulfilment of Old Testament writings. Therefore, if the New Testament completes the Old and contains all the hallmarks of being inspired by the same Spirit, it should surely be called 'Scripture' as well.

Indeed, Jesus is the living Word of God (1 John 1:1-4), who came to fulfill the Laws, Psalms, and Prophecies of the Old Testament (Matt. 5:17, Luke 24:44-49). The Word of God is one unit because there is one God who commissioned it, one Man who epitomized it and one Spirit who inspired it (see: Eph. 4:3-6). And so, as one reads the Word more, one can understand the Holy Spirit more.

There is one book of the Bible which speaks more of the Holy Spirit than any other. This book is 'The Acts of the Apostles'. By looking at the table further back, it is clear that there are roughly as many references to the Holy Spirit in Acts as there are in the four Gospels combined. This emphasis on the work of the Spirit in Acts has led to some suggesting that it should be called 'The Acts of the Holy Spirit'. Therefore, that book is a good place to start as we now delve deeper into studying this important subject.

The Book of Acts chronicles the early church of Christ and serves as a sequel to Luke's Gospel about the life of Christ. He begins in chapter 1 of Acts by recording the risen Christ's command to His disciples to remain in Jerusalem until they received the power of the promised Holy Spirit. That power would enable them to spread the Gospel of the Kingdom to the ends of the Earth. Luke says that just before His ascension back to Heaven, Christ spoke "through the Holy Spirit" when He said these things and that His disciples would be "baptized in the Holy Spirit not many days [later]." (see: verses 1-9).

In chapter 2, Luke then describes this baptism of the Spirit, which occurred on the Jewish Festival of Pentecost. It is so named, because it refers to a 50th day after something - the root 'pent' referring to five, e.g. pentagon, pentathlon. 50 is of course five multiplied by ten. Pentecost was the 50th day from Passover.

Pentecost was originally called the 'Festival of Weeks' and was celebrated to remember when God gave Moses the Law on Mount Sinai. This took place 50 days after the Passover and their escape from

Egypt. For 40 days Moses led them away from Egypt and then in obedience to God, he left them to wait for God Mount Sinai. On the 10th day of being on the mountain (50 days after Passover), God came down in fire and gave him the Ten Commandments (see: Exodus 12-23).

Zooming forward to about 29 AD and 50 days after that years' Passover (when Jesus died and rose again), the risen Christ spent 40 days with the early Christians and then told them to wait on Mount Zion for the power of God to come down. And 10 days later, the Holy Spirit comes down in fire and fills all the believers with the power of God! This was 50 days after the Passover. Therefore, on the day the Jews celebrate the giving of the Law, the people were given the Spirit.

In addition to the 12 disciples, there were a further 108 or so believers (120 in total) who waited patiently and prayerfully as one unified body and when they were gathered together on Pentecost Sunday they hear:

> "a [heavenly] sound like a mighty rushing wind, and it
> filled the entire house where they were sitting. And
> divided tongues as of fire appeared to them and rested
> on each one of them. And they were all filled with the
> Holy Spirit and began to speak in other tongues as the
> Spirit gave them utterance..."

> Acts 2:2-4

Straight away, thousands of people from all over run to find out what's going on, as they encounter amazing sounds and wonders! People from other parts hear their own languages being spoken by these new Spirit-filled believers, who are speaking in tongues (verses 5-13). Peter boldly proclaims to the growing crowds, telling them that this was what was prophesied by the Prophet Joel in the Old Testament (see: verses 14-37). He encourages the people to repent, commit to Christ, get baptised in water and they would receive the Holy Spirit, just as he and the 120 believers did.

3,000 were converted to Christ and received the promised Holy Spirit in one day, with more being added all the time as the disciples committed themselves to prayer, the Word, worship, communion and sharing their possessions (verses 38-47). Contrast this to the record in Exodus, when 3,000 people were killed due to worshipping the golden calf, instead of patiently waiting for Moses to come down the mountain with the promised Law (see: Exod. 32).

This dramatic and earth-shattering event marks the birth of what we now call 'the Church'. God arranged to send His Spirit on this big feast of Pentecost causing many to "see and fear, and put their trust in the LORD" (Psa. 40:3) for generations to come. Throughout Acts, we read of how the church goes from strength to strength, growing and maturing and continually being led and empowered by the Holy Spirit who enables the believers to boldly declare the Word of God. The church knew the truth, but needed that truth empowered by God Himself - through His Spirit.

Later, in the second half of Acts, Luke tells us of when the Apostle Paul visited a group of new Christians in Ephesus. Paul asks this group if they had received the Holy Spirit who had been poured out in Jerusalem. They say,

…we don't know what you mean. What is the Holy Spirit?

see: Acts 19:1-7

Earlier, Paul had visited a group of Greek Jews called the Bereans. He preached the Gospel to them and we read that:

…they received the message with great eagerness and examined the Scriptures every day to see if what Paul said was true"

See: Acts 17:10-15

We also read in the Gospels that Jesus Himself continually referred back to the scriptures and that He opened their minds and hearts of his listeners to them (see: Matt. 12, Luke 24:25-26, 44-49; John 5:46-47). That is what this book is all about. So that:

- **like the Ephesian believers - I will ask who and what is the Holy Spirit**

- **like the Berean believers - I will search the scriptures in order to get the right answers**

- like Peter - I will challenge myself and all readers about what all this means for our lives

- like Paul - I will encourage each reader to receive the Holy Spirit more fully into their lives

All this helps us to bring the Word and the Spirit together in our understanding. Just as the Word tells us of the Spirit, so too the Spirit points us back to the Word. The Word can also refer to Christ who is the living Word of God and eventually draws us back to an intimate relationship with the Father.

The Co-Creator

Both Moses who wrote Genesis and John who wrote the fourth Gospel begin their respective books with reference to the creation of the universe. If we compare Genesis 1:1-5 with John 1:1-5 we see the work of the Father, the Son (the Word) and the Spirit in creation. Here is a table to demonstrate it:

GENESIS 1 - THE PHYSICAL THINGS CREATED BY A SPIRITUAL BEING	JOHN 1 - THE SPIRITUAL THINGS CREATED BY THE ONE WHO BECAME PHYSICAL FLESH
"In the Beginning" (v1)	"In the Beginning" (v1)
"the Spirit of God was hovering" and was with God (v2).	"was the Word, and the Word was with God, the Word was God" that is Jesus (v1)
"Then God said..."	"through Him"...the Word (v3)
"Let there be light!" & life was created on the third day (v3,11)	"In Him was life, and the life was the light of men" (v4)
"God divided the light from the darkness" (v4)	"the light shines in the darkness and the darkness did not comprehend /overcome it" (v5)

As one can see, God said let 'us' make man in 'our image' (Gen. 1:26). Seen as nothing in all creation was made without the Son and the Spirit as well (as those comparative verses show), the 'us' and the 'our' must refer to them. The Father is speaking to them. This shows their divine equality.

Though we are different to God and not equal to Him either, we have been made in His image and so will be like Him in some ways. For example, we are a tri-part being - body, soul and spirit, and He God is Father, Son and Spirit. Many find the concept of the Trinity difficult to accept - that there can be one God, yet three persons who are all equally God. Yet each human in the world has a body, a soul and spirit and yet is still just one being. In this comparative light, some might say, Jesus is the Body (as He became flesh), the Spirit is comparable to our spirit and the Father is like the soul.

Indeed, the Bible does say God has a soul (Lev. 26:11, Jer. 32:41), yet we have to be careful of this comparison as it doesn't quite fit. The reference to Him having a soul (and also others which say He has a back, arms, hands, a side and feet) may just be anthropomorphic language (being described with human features) to help us understand Him better from our limited perspective.

I believe it is very important we also remember that we are not mini gods. The scriptures that seem to say humans are gods are actually meant sarcastically in regard to rulers who considered themselves 'mighty imperious' over everyone else (see: Psa. 82) and John 10:22-42).

After all, the lie Satan sold Eve was that both she and her husband could be just like God and know all things (Gen. 3). God is Spirit and spirits do not have bodies. In fact, God is described as invisible in scripture (see: Col. 1:15, 1 Tim. 1:17 and Heb. 11:27). Until Christ (the image of the Father) came in the flesh, no part of the Godhead had a body and yet He made us with a body! So, we can see there that we are different to Him in that very fundamental way and in other ways too.

Getting back to similarities between us and Godhead is that we have thoughts, words and actions. The Father *thought* of the creation (He decided to make the world - Jas. 1:18), the Son was *the Word* of Creation (the 'saying' part - "God said Let there be light" - Jesus is the light and the spoken Word - John 1:1-14) and the Spirit was the action part of the initial thought (Ps. 104:30; 1 Cor. 2:11). It is impossible to fully explain and to understand, but it is one which is still true from studying God's written Word.

After a summary of how God created the world (Gen. 1), we read that He 'breathed' life into the first man - Adam (Gen. 2:7). In the scriptures, the 'breath of God' always refers to the Holy Spirit:

- Job 33:4 says, "...the Spirit of God has made me, and the breath of the Almighty gives me life".
- Psalm 33:6 says, "By the word of the LORD the heavens were made, their starry host by the breath of his mouth."
- Jesus (the Word) breathed on His disciples and said, "receive the Holy Spirit" (John 20:22).

Following Pentecost when the Spirit literally breathed down on the first Christians (Acts 2), Luke tells us of another group of Christians who "were all filled with the Holy Spirit and spoke the word of God boldly" (Acts 4:31). Then later still in Acts 15, Luke tells us about a Christian Council held in Jerusalem for the leaders to discuss a theological issue. The members see that what they felt the Spirit was showing them and what the scriptures said agreed with each other and so must be on the right tracks.

Again and again, we see the Word and Spirit coming together in unison, bringing about the new things the Father wants to make in us and through us.

His Divine Equality

To live a more complete spiritual life, we must know God as Father, Son *and* Spirit. I believe this needs further unpacking. To do this, I would like to take you through the New Testament from beginning to end. This will hopefully convey to you more than you've known before the divine equality the Spirit has with the Father and the Son. By the same token, this hopefully makes clear to us that knowing Him more leads us that fuller life of faith that Jesus promised (John 10:10).

Jesus shows His disciples that new believers must be sealed in the name and power of God as Father, Son and Spirit:

> Therefore go and make disciples of all nations, baptising them in the name of the Father and of the Son and of the Holy Spirit.

> Matthew 28:19

These sacred words of Christ clearly show us that there is authority in the name of the Holy Spirit - and an authority which is equal to that found in the name of the Father and of the Son. We can also see from this passage that it is vital for potential disciples to believe in God as a triune being, and that this be a part of their initiation into the Kingdom through the rite of baptism.

Recording the record of Christ's baptism, we see Him; the Spirit's power resting on Him and the Father's assuring and approving voice speaking over Him:

When all the people were being baptised, Jesus was baptised too. And as he was praying, heaven was opened and the Holy Spirit descended on him in bodily form like a dove. And a voice came from heaven: 'You are my Son, whom I love; with you I am well pleased.'

Luke 3:21-23

In the light of that, consider these words of Christ:

Jesus answered, 'Very truly I tell you, no one can enter the kingdom of God unless they are born of water and the Spirit. Flesh gives birth to flesh, but the Spirit gives birth to spirit. You should not be surprised at my saying, "You must be born again." The wind blows wherever it pleases. You hear its sound, but you cannot tell where it comes from or where it is going. So it is with everyone born of the Spirit...For God so loved the world that he gave his one and only Son, that whoever believes in him shall not perish but have eternal life... For he whom God has sent utters the words of God, for he gives the Spirit without measure. The Father loves the Son and has given all things into his hand. Whoever believes in the Son has eternal life...

John 3:5-8, 16, 34-36

Just as the New Testament makes clear that belief in the Triune God should be at the heart of all travellers on the way of salvation, the scriptures also invoke the persons of the Trinity when warning about veering off the straight and narrow way. The Book of Hebrews especially makes this point. The writer refers to the danger of those once being sanctified by God ignoring His will, neglecting His salvation, trampling His Son underfoot and insulting the Spirit of Grace (see: 2:3-4; 3:7-15; 6:1-6; 9:14; 10:5-16 and 26-31).

In the following passages taken from John's Gospel, Jesus explains the relationship between the persons of the Trinity, and between the Trinity and the Christian. One will also notice that how Jesus refers to the Spirit as 'he' and 'him' several times. The Apostle Paul followed this convention when he said (see: Romans 8:16-17).

In the first example from John, Jesus acknowledges Himself as the disciple's Advocate (or Counsellor) before the Father / the go-between / the one who makes the way:

> I will ask the Father, and he will give you another advocate to help you and be with you for ever – the Spirit of truth.
>
> John 14:16

In a court case, you need an advocate or counsellor to advise and mediate before the judge, just as we have one Advocate and Mediator - Jesus Christ (1 Tim. 2:5, 1 John 2:1), who operates on our behalf before God the Father - our Judge. In fact, the Father now judges through Christ (John 5:22, Acts 17:31).

Getting back to the passage, Jesus is explaining that He will ask the Father to send another one <u>like</u> (the same as) Himself - the Holy Spirit. He is the Spirit of Christ Himself - an Advocate for all believers, just as Jesus was when He was on Earth in the flesh. Jesus remains our Advocate, but that role is now done through the Spirit. Just as He is our intercessor before the Father, but the Spirit also intercedes through us (Rom. 8:34, 26).

We needed an advocate because we have all sinned and fallen short of God's perfection and holiness, resulting in spiritual death and separation from our perfect, holy Father (Rom. 3:23; 6:23, Col. 1:21-22). Our own sin condemns us, yet God the Father in His love and mercy sent us His Son to pay the price for our sin by dying in our place on the cross and by raising back to life to offer us eternal life after we die.

If we confess our sins and believe in Him both in word and in our heart, we are saved from judgment, condemnation, Hell and eternal death. Instead, we receive the promise of eternal life and this is done by His Spirit coming to reside within us (please see: John 3:16-17 and Rom. 8:11).

Back in John 14, Jesus continues:

The world cannot accept <u>him</u>, because it neither sees him nor knows him. But you know him, for he lives <u>with you</u> (now) and <u>will be in you</u> (soon).

John 14:17

Though we cannot see the Holy Spirit, we can see His effect in our own lives as well as in the lives of other Christians, just as we can see the effect of the wind blowing through trees. That is how "it is with everyone [who is] born of the Spirit" (John 3:8). We believe by faith and not be sight (2 Cor. 5:7). Notice in the passage just above how Jesus shows the difference between the Spirit just being *with* them, and the Spirit being *in* them in the future. That was a prophetic reference to the Spirit's outpouring and infilling at Pentecost.

It shows that there's a difference between being *influenced* by the Spirit and being *baptised* in the Spirit. Up until the festival of Pentecost that occurred just after Christ's ascension, the Holy Spirit would only usually *be with* a person and rarely *in* them, but as Joel prophesied, one day, the Spirit would be poured out *into* all believers (Joel 2:28-32, Acts 2:16-21)! Moses also longed for a day when this would happen (see: Num. 11), but this would not occur until after Son had come first to make a way for this to happen.

Jesus shares that:

When the <u>Advocate</u> comes, whom I will send to you from the <u>Father</u> – <u>the Spirit</u> of truth who goes out from the <u>Father – he will testify about me</u>…<u>when he, the Spirit</u> of truth, comes, he will guide you into all the truth. He will not speak on his own; he will speak only what he hears, and he will tell you what is yet to come. He will glorify me because it is from me that he will receive what he will make known to you. <u>All that belongs to the Father is mine. That is why I said the Spirit will receive from me</u> what he will make known to you.

John 15:26; 16:12-15

There was much controversy in the early church as to whether the Holy Spirit proceeded from the Father alone or from the Son as well. To me, the above two verses and the words of Acts 2:32-33 and Revelation 5:6 show that the Spirit "proceeds from the Father and the Son" as per the words of the Nicene Creed, completed in 381AD. The fall out between the Western and Eastern churches was greatly widened over just a few words, resulting in what is now known as the 'Filioque controversy'.

The Latin term 'Filioque' describes the dual procession of the Spirit. There is no English equivalent, so in the Nicene Creed statement of faith we read:

> We believe in the Holy Spirit, the Lord, the giver of life, who proceeds from the Father <u>and the Son</u>. With the Father and the Son he is worshiped and glorified.

(Church of England, 2016)

The Eastern church rejected the notion that the Spirit proceeded from the Son as well, whereas the Western church wanted it kept in (Filioque, 2016). The Devil would want nothing more than for Christians to argue over their core beliefs. Ironically, that is one of the reasons why we need the Holy Spirit. He guides us into all truth, helps us to understand the Word more and by praying in Him we form a guard against the accuser, deceiver and confuser - aka. the Devil.

Moving on from the Gospels, we come to the Book of Acts. I will not major on it here, as it has been and will be touched on a lot throughout this book. Yet, one example of a Trinitarian verse in Acts I will provide here comes from a significant turning point in the early church - the trail and stoning of Stephen. This event radically upped the ante of Christian persecution.

Stephen was the first Christian martyr in world history and despite finding himself falsely accused of blasphemy and about to be stoned to death, we read these wonderful words about what he saw and said:

> But Stephen, <u>full of the Holy Spirit</u>, looked up to heaven and saw <u>the glory of God, and</u> Jesus standing at the right hand of God. 'Look,' he said, 'I see heaven open and the <u>Son of Man standing at the right hand of God</u>.'...While they were stoning him, Stephen prayed, '<u>Lord Jesus</u>, receive my spirit.' Then he fell on his knees and cried out, '<u>Lord</u>, do not hold this sin against them.' When he had said this, he fell asleep.

> Acts 7:51-60

There are clear parallels here to the trial and death of Jesus, who was falsely accused of blasphemy, and when being put to death asked the Father to receive His spirit and forgive those around Him. Yet, Stephen asked 'Jesus' to receive His Spirit. This points to Christ's equality with the Father. Christ is seen standing side by side with the Father in Heaven. And it is the Spirit who infills Stephen and allows Him to see this hopeful scene, even at the point of death.

Yes, this passage has doubtless given hope to persecuted Christians throughout the years who have followed Stephen into martyrdom. As with Stephen, God's Spirit is with them until the end and like him they will be received into the arms of Christ when they pass from this evil world into His glorious Kingdom.

Here, we now move onto the letters and epistles of the Bible. Paul's letter to the believers in Rome refers extensively to the work of the Spirit, but we will come onto that later. Paul closes his second letter to the church in Corinth with these famous words:

> May the grace of the Lord Jesus Christ, and the love of God (the Father), and the fellowship of the Holy Spirit be with you all.

2 Corinthians 13:14

That verse of blessing has now been called 'the Grace' in Christian circles and also acts as a mini creed too. The words resemble Christ's closing words at the end of Matthew's Gospel (quoted above) that all believers must be baptised into the Father, the Son and the Spirit. Both Christ's words there and Paul's closing words here tell us again of divine Trinitarian equality.

In Ephesians, Paul also refers to their being one Father, one Lord (which usually applies to Jesus in the New Testament) and one Spirit in the same sentence (see: Eph. 4:2-6, which is quoted in the Introduction). In fact, many of the introductions to the letters of the New Testament incorporate words on the Father, the Son and the

Spirit. As with Jesus, it would seem the writers were keen for their recipients to have that Trinitarian understanding at the forefront of their theology and active faith.

Indeed, Ephesians is no exception, for in the seventieth verse, Paul says:

> I keep asking that the God of our Lord Jesus Christ, the glorious Father, may give you the Spirit of wisdom and revelation, so that you may know him better.

> Ephesians 1:17

Notice that he says that he "keeps asking". He says later in Ephesians to pray in the Spirit "continually" (see: 6:18). For we must have the Spirit residing in our inner man in order to know Christ better. You cannot have intimacy with Him without His Spirit convicting, counselling and comforting you along your journey.

In his introduction to his letter to the Colossian church, Paul says that he always "thank[s] God the Father" for the Colossians' "faith in Christ Jesus" and he shares how he is blessed by their "love in the Spirit" (see: Col. 1:1-7). Likewise, Peter opens His first letter by stating that his readers have been:

> ...chosen according to the foreknowledge of God the Father, through the sanctifying work of the Spirit, to be obedient to Jesus Christ and sprinkled with his blood.

> See: 1 Peter 1:1-2

And look at John's words in his first letter:

> This is the one who came by water and blood – Jesus Christ. He did not come by water only, but by water and blood. And it is the Spirit who testifies, because the Spirit is the truth. **For there are three that testify in heaven: the Father, the Word and the Holy Spirit, and these three are one. And** there are three that testify on earth: the Spirit, the water and the blood; and the three are in agreement.
>
> 1 John 5:7-8
>
> (it should be noted that some manuscripts don't contain the words in **bold**)

Finally, near the end of the Bible, John greets His readers with these powerful words:

> Grace and peace to you
> <u>from him</u> who is, and who was, and who is to come, and
> <u>from the Seven-fold Spirit</u> before his throne, and
> <u>from Jesus Christ</u>…the ruler of the kings of the earth.
>
> Revelation 1:4-5
>
> (see also verse 8)

So, there we have a blessing of grace and peace from the Father, from the Spirit and from the Son. Then three chapters later, he shares a vision of God on the throne, where all the angels, creatures and people of Heaven never cease to praise Him as the triune God:

Day and night they never stop saying: "Holy, holy, holy is the Lord God Almighty," who was, and is, and is to come...Then I saw <u>a Lamb</u>, looking as if it had been slain, standing at the centre of the throne, [he] had seven horns and seven eyes, which is <u>the seven-fold Spirit of God</u> sent out into all the earth...Then I heard every creature in heaven and on earth and under the earth and on the sea, and all that is in them, saying: '<u>To him who sits on the throne and to the Lamb</u> be praise and honour and glory and power, for ever and ever!'

Revelation 4:8; 5:6,13

There, John is being shown an image of God to help Him understand the Godhead. See how he hears everyone giving praise to "him who sits on the throne" which is surely the Father, because he then says, "<u>and</u> to the Lamb" which of course is Jesus (John 1:29). Earlier he refers to the Lamb having seven eyes, which represented the "seven-fold Spirit of God" - the Holy Spirit. So, all of Heaven are worshipping the Father, the Son and also the Spirit of the Son who has been commissioned to go out from the Father and the Son into all the Earth.

All those in Heaven sing "Holy, holy, holy" to God, because He a holy Father (John 17:11), who has a holy Son (Luke 1:35) from whom comes the Holy Spirit (Acts 2:33, 38. See also: 1 Pet. 1:13-16). Isaiah saw a similar scene in his early ministry where everyone in Heaven was singing "Holy, holy, holy" to the One on the throne. In fact, John takes those very words from Isaiah to show that he saw and heard the same thing (see: Isa. 6).

In fact, Isaiah emphasises the holiness of God more so than any other writer in the Bible. Perhaps this is why God could reveal more of His holiness. Isaiah refers to the Father as holy (10:20; 63:15-16), the Son as holy (53:9-11) and the Spirit as holy (63:10-11), Isaiah contains two of the only three references to the Spirit bring the Holy Spirit in the whole of the Old Testament. The other occurrence is in Psalm 51:11.

God is the same in both the Old and the New Testament. He is holy, holy, holy and worthy of all our praise and adoration! It is to a holy God we submit and by knowing His Holy Spirit we too become holy, just as He is holy - this is our highest calling and should be our greatest desire (1 Pet. 1:14-16). For Christ didn't just die on the cross to forgive us, He did to make us holy, so we could come boldly before our Heavenly Father (Heb. 10:22). It is the Spirit's role to remind us of how we've been forgiven, but also to counsel and convict us of any unholiness in our lives too (Rom. 8:11-16).

His Divine Worthiness

The fact that the Bible so regularly calls the Spirit 'holy' in a similar way to that of the Father and the Son (i.e. with a capital 'H'), surely implies an equal status and therefore worthy of worship and adoration. We also read how all those in Heaven emphasise the holiness of God in their worship, whereby they sing "Holy, holy, holy" (Isa. 6:1-4, Rev. 4). This triple use of this attribute might be in reference to the Trinity. In light of this, I believe that the Holy Spirit is to be worshipped here on Earth as well by all those who truly know God.

As with all the Psalms, the 95th one is a worship song to God, but this one also includes firm warnings from God about sin and rebellion. The writer of Hebrews quotes large chunks of Psalm 95 and states that it was the Holy Spirit giving the warnings in that Psalm: "So, as the Holy Spirit says, 'Today, if you hear his voice, do not harden your hearts...'" (see: Heb. 3:7-11; 10:15-18). As I said, this Psalm also praises God, therefore, the God spoken of in that Psalm is the Holy Spirit, and by the same token, is also clearly worthy of worship. Indeed, the word 'worship' means 'worth-ship'. He is entitled to it just as a King has 'kingship' and a Lord has 'lordship'. He is worth it!

Similarly, at the end of Acts, Paul addresses a group of Jewish leaders with these words: "The Holy Spirit spoke the truth to your ancestors when he said through Isaiah the prophet: "'Go to this people and say, "You will be ever hearing but never understanding; you will be ever seeing but never perceiving... Otherwise [they might] turn, and I would heal them.'"" (see: Acts 28:25-27, see also: Isaiah 6:9-10).

In the original passage in Isaiah, it is in fact the Lord God and Father who was speaking, but here, Paul is saying it was the Spirit. To me, this is not a contradiction, but rather, a glimpse into the mysterious, intertwined relationships and unity within the Godhead. It also demonstrates that God speaks to man through His Spirit and therefore without His Spirit people will not be able to "hear with their ears" and understand His will.

Notice, it was a passage from Isaiah 6 that Paul was quoting there - the very same chapter where we read of all the Heavenly beings singing, "Holy, holy, holy" to God (as quoted above). This shows that the Spirit is being worshipped too, for it was He who was speaking there, as Paul says. So, we see the Father and the Spirit, but what about the Son? Well, the Book of Isaiah is filled with references to "the Holy One" which refer to God the Father (see: 12:6, 30:12,15; 48:17), but wee elsewhere that Jesus is given this title too (see: Psa. 16:10, Luke 1:35, Acts 2:27; 13:35).

Moving back to the divine worthiness of the Spirit - we read in 1 Peter 4:14 that:

> "If you are reproached for the name of Christ, blessed are you, for <u>the Spirit of glory</u> and of God rests upon you. On their part <u>He is blasphemed</u>, but on your part <u>He is glorified</u>."

Even though Peter appears to be saying that it is Christ who 'is glorified', He nevertheless calls the Holy Spirit 'the Spirit of glory', which surely means He is worthy of glorification - He is to be glorified (see also: 1 Cor. 3:7-8, 16-18). Jesus said that the Spirit can be blasphemed (see: Mark 3:29), just as God as Father and Son can be. Therefore, this verse could apply to blaspheming the Spirit as well as glorying Him.

Jesus also said that "God is Spirit" (capital S in many translations) and "those who worship Him must worship in spirit and truth" (see: John 4:23-24). Some translations say "must worship him in the Spirit" (see the NIV, NLT and KJV renderings).

So why doesn't the Bible clearly state that we should worship the Spirit, just as it states we can worship the Father and the Son?

Though there wasn't the understanding of the Trinity (the Godhead) in the Old Testament as in the New Testament, when people were worshipping God then, they were perhaps unknowingly worshipping God as Father, Son and Spirit anyway. Despite the aforesaid lack of explicit verses about worshipping the Spirit, there aren't too many about worshipping the Son either. Though Jesus received worship whilst on Earth (Matt. 2:11; 28:9, John 12:13), He came to empty Himself of the glory He had in Heaven and became that humble servant (Mark 10:45, Phil. 2:7), just as the Spirit now is operating as Christ did when He was on Earth - as a humble servant, but also one who is worthy of worship.

It was in fact Jesus Himself who explained that we should worship God, who "is Spirit" and worship Him "in (the) Spirit" (John 4:23-24) as referred to above. In addition, the scriptures call us to pray "in the Spirit" at all times and particularly in private (Eph. 6:20,

Jude 0:20), so therefore, the Spirit is very much about us and our relationship with God. He takes a humble, sacrificial role for our sake in order to the lead us back to God the Father and the Son (John 14:16).

Jesus said that He glorified the Father, and that the Spirit would glorify Him (see: John 16:14; 17:1). The Spirit is supposed to fill us just as God's presence filled the Temple when it was first built and remained there in the inner sanctuary (2 Chr. 7:1), so there's a danger that we might start focusing too inwardly if we learn too early about worshipping God as the Holy Spirit. There's also a danger that we segregate the Godhead into three gods, when there is only one God of three persons.

Perhaps this is why there are no verses which explicitly say to worship the Spirit and why also so few hymn writers have written songs which make mention of worshipping the Spirit. There are however enough passages quoted above, which clearly show the Spirit is God and is *so* worthy of praise, glory, honour and worship. I believe we should acknowledge the Spirit more in worship, but in conjunction with that, also have more teaching about Him and His role in our lives to make sure we do not become inwardly-focused.

His Divine Attributes

It is commonly accepted that for any being to be considered divine, they must fulfil the following criteria:

- **omnipresent** - ever-present / can be present everywhere at the same time
- **omniscient** - all-seeing / all-knowing
- **omnipotent** - all-powerful / has unlimited power

In the Bible, we learn that God the Father and God the Son have those attributes (see: Psa. 139:4,7, Isa. 46:9-10, Matt. 9:4; 10:29-30, Acts 1:24, Eph. 3:20, Heb. 1:3, 1 John 3:20), but can this be said of the Spirit of God?

I believe the answer is a resounding "yes"! Let me expand those three bullet points and prove it through scripture.

- **He is omnipresent** - ever-present / can be present everywhere at the same time

For the Psalmist said,

Where can I go from your Spirit? Where can I flee from your presence?

Psalm 139:7

Luke records an example of the Spirit working in different locations:

*The Spirit told Philip, 'Go to that chariot and stay near it.'...
[later] the Spirit of the Lord suddenly took Philip away, and
the eunuch did not see him again, but went on his way
rejoicing. Philip, however, appeared at Azotus...Paul and his
companions travelled throughout the region of Phrygia and
Galatia, having been kept by the Holy Spirit from preaching
the word in the province of Asia.*

See: Acts 8:26-40; 16:6

- **He is omniscient** - all-seeing / all-knowing

For Jesus said:

*All that belongs to the Father is mine. That is why I said the
Spirit will receive from me what he will make known to you.*

John 16:15

Paul goes further by explaining:

*...as it is written: 'What no eye has seen, what no ear has
heard, and what no human mind has conceived' — the things
God has prepared for those who love him — these are the things
God has revealed to us by his Spirit. The Spirit searches all
things, even the deep things of God. For who knows a person's
thoughts except their own spirit within them? In the same way*

no one knows the thoughts of God except the Spirit of God. What we have received is not the spirit of the world, but the Spirit who is from God, so that we may understand what God has freely given us.

1 Corinthians 2:9-12.
See also: Isaiah 64:4

- **He is omnipotent** - all-powerful / has unlimited power

For as the prophet Zechariah said:

This is the word of the Lord...Not by (man's) might, nor by (man's) power, but by my Spirit, says the Lord of hosts.

Zechariah 4:6
(Words in brackets added)

Luke records the annunciation of Christ's incarnation:

...Mary said to the angel, "How will this be, since I am a virgin?" And the angel answered her, "The Holy Spirit will come upon you, and the power of the Most High will overshadow you; therefore the child to be born will be called holy - the Son of God.

Luke 1:34-35

Paul explains:

[Jesus] was declared to be the Son of God in power according to the Spirit. If the Spirit of him who raised Jesus from the dead dwells in you, he who raised Christ Jesus from the dead will also give life to your mortal bodies through his Spirit who dwells in you...May the God of hope fill you with all joy and peace in believing, so that by the power of the Holy Spirit you may abound in hope.

Romans 1:4; 8:11; 15:13

As with the Father and with the Son, the scriptures say that the Spirit is "eternal" (see: Isa. 9:6, Heb. 9:14; 13:8).

Throughout the New Testament, the use of 'God' usually refers to the Father; the use of 'Lord' usually refers to the Son and the use of 'Spirit' (with a capital 'S') obviously refers to the Holy Spirit. We see a clear example of this in one short passage:

There are different kinds of gifts, but <u>the same Spirit</u> distributes them.

There are different kinds of service, but <u>the same Lord</u>.

There are different kinds of working, but in all of them and in everyone it is <u>the same God</u> at work.

1 Corinthians 12:4-6 (gaps added for emphasis)

Paul is teaching us that there are many kinds of gifts, service and working, but that they all come from the same source, as in "the same Spirit", "the same Lord" and "the same God". Indeed, the Spirit gives the gifts, which enable us to serve the Son, which is work unto the Father. So, the Father, the Son and the Spirit are clearly one and "the same" God, as is evident by their many shared divine attributes seen in the passages above, but also in their complementary roles as seen in the passage here and in many others also. One can see the Tri-unity of God.

Though God the Father is frequently called "the Lord" (especially in the Old Testament) and Jesus is called as such (in the New Testament), moreover, the Spirit is also referred to as "the Lord" as well. In 2 Corinthians 3:17, Paul states, "<u>Now the Lord is the Spirit</u>, and where the Spirit of the Lord is, there is freedom."

Paul opens up his letter to the Galatian church by teaching us that the Father raised Jesus from the dead, but in Romans, he says the Spirit raised Jesus from the dead (see: Rom. 8:11; Gal. 1:1. See also: 1 Pet. 1:20-21; 3:18).

Isaiah 63:10 says that the Holy Spirit can be sinned against. Furthermore, in Acts we see an example of this, when the Apostle Peter confronted a married couple over a sin they had both committed:

Peter said, "Ananias, why has Satan filled your heart to lie to the Holy Spirit...? Why have you conceived this thing in your heart? You have not lied to men but to God." and to Ananias' wife Peter said, "How could you conspire to test the Spirit of the Lord?"

See: Acts 5:3-9

Peter's encounter with Ananias and his wife demonstrates to us that sinning against the Holy Spirit or putting Him to the test is the same as sinning against God or putting Him to the test, respectively (see: Deut. 6:16, Luke 4:12), because the Holy Spirit *is* God. Similarly, the writer of Psalm 106 refers to when the Israelites angered the Lord and therefore rebelled against His Spirit (see: Exod. 17:7, Psa. 106:32-33).

As we have to remember, God is our Father, who has a Son and a Spirit, who are also Him, in the sense they are God as well. It is a reality to wonderful to adequately explain, yet it does not mean it is untrue.

Here is a portion of a prayer called *St. Patrick's Breastplate*, which I believe can help us to understand the Trinity more:

I bind unto myself today,
the strong Name of the Trinity,
by invocation of the same,
the Three in One, and One in Three.

(Wikipedia, 2016)

He or someone else was purported to have used the Irish shamrock to better explain the nature Trinity - one leaf, but also three.

The belief in the Trinity is often criticised by Muslims, who are concerned we are worshiping three gods. They believe 'Allah' is One and not 'Three in One' as St. Patrick and the Bible indicate. They, like Christians believe their God is the source of all love and also the creator of all things, yet, I would say that if God is only 'One' and not 'Three in One', who then was He loving before He made the world and everyone in it? Love only exists between two or more people. It has no purpose if it is not shared.

I believe that the relationship between the three persons of the Godhead help to explain why God made the world in the first place. The Father so enjoyed the eternal fellowship He had with His Son and with the Spirit that He decided to create a larger family. And so, we are called His sons and daughters who have Jesus as our elder brother and the Spirit as our helper - who shows us how to live like our perfect elder brother and ultimately lead us back into the loving arms of our heavenly Father. All of this can be seen in the infamous eighth chapter of Romans alone, yet there are other relevant passages worth reading about too (Mark 3:34, John 3:16; 14:16, Gal. 4:4-5 and Heb. 2:11).

The fact that the Trinity (or Godhead) is far from easy to understand or explain is something leading atheist, Richard Dawkins uses to attack Christianity. In his infamous work, *The God Delusion*, he labels the doctrine of the Trinity as "sophistry" (Dawkins, 2006). In other words, he believes that it is a made-up belief system designed to be sophisticated in order to look spiritual and divinely inspired. Yet, he cannot adequately explain the Universe! It is a reality too complex to fully comprehend or explain sufficiently, yet it is real.

If we could understand and explain everything about God, He wouldn't be God, would He? Likewise, if we could understand and explain everything in the Bible, it would not be so divine, or any greater than any other book in the world. It is the mystery of God, His Word and His universe that shows me that they are all beyond our human minds. If anything, it humbles me.

How could our finite, limited minds ever hope to explain the infinite, unlimited Creator of the universe? Yet, God shares so much about His character through the Word and through His Spirit here on Earth.

For from him and through him and for him are all things. To him be the glory forever! Amen.

Romans 11:36

His Divine Personhood

One important thing we must remember about the Holy Spirit is that He not an "it", or a force, like 'the Force' in *Star Wars*. No, our Lord Jesus described both His Father and the Spirit by using personal pronouns - "he" and "him":

> ...I will ask the Father, and <u>he</u> will give you another Helper to be with you for ever, even the Spirit of truth, whom the world cannot receive, because it neither sees <u>him</u> nor knows <u>him</u>. You know <u>him</u>, for <u>he</u> dwells with you and will be in you...
>
> John 14:14-17

A few verses down and Jesus also says that the Spirit would be our personal comforter and counsellor (see: vs. 26 in a few translations).

Paul says that the Spirit thinks and knows (1 Cor. 2:10), that He loves us (Rom. 15:30) that we can also have fellowship with Him (2 Cor. 13:14), but that He can be grieved, offended, insulted and His fire can be quenched in us due to our sins (Eph. 4:30, 1 Thes. 5:19, see also: Heb. 10:29). He prays for and through us (Rom. 8:26, Jude 0:20), He teaches us (Luke 12:12), He personally warns people; He prompts them and has a voice that calls out to people. We are strongly encouraged to listen to His voice (2 Sam. 23:2, Acts 20:22-24, 1 Tim. 4:1, Heb. 3:7-19; Rev. 2:7). All this shows that He is a person and a person that we can be close to.

His Role with the Father

He is the Spirit of the Father who gives us words to say when we trust in Him (Matt. 10:20). He is the Spirit of Jesus Christ who prevents us from harm if we listen, and so this will draw us to understanding Christ better (Acts 16:7, Rom. 8:9-11, Eph. 1:17). He convicts us of sin (Neh. 9:30, John 16:8), grants us spiritual freedom (Rom. 8:1-27, 2 Cor. 3:17), renews and strengthens our spirit (Eph. 3:16, Tis. 3:5), leads us on level ground (Psa. 143:10, Gal. 5:25) and sanctifies us so we can be holy just as our Father God is holy (1 Pet. 1:2, 16).

As established earlier, He inspired the writing of the Word of God, its many prophecies and brings them to mind for the believer and so this brings us closer to God (John 14:26, 2 Tim. 3:16, 2 Pet. 1:21).

When Jesus was baptised in the River Jordan, the Father spoke from Heaven and the Spirit descended on Jesus in bodily form. This shows that the Spirit isn't just the Spirit of the Father and the Son (just an aspect of their being - e.g. an entity, a representation of them), but He is His own person with a role to fulfil (Luke 3:21-22). He comes and enters a person to anoint them, guide them and help them. The baptism of Jesus was an event that showed the Father, the Son and the Spirit together as one, but also as three distinct persons.

So, the Holy Spirit *is* God, but He is also the third person of the Godhead:

- **The Father** sets perfect standards and establishes what is right and wrong.

- **The Son** is demonstrated those perfect standards by always doing what was right – He is the very epitome of what God wants in us.

- **The Spirit** is there to give is the strength and energy to be like the Son and lead us back to the Father. He does this by confirming within us that we are adopted sons and daughters of the Father and therefore brothers and sisters of the Son.

This can be seen in how Jesus described God as the Father of truth (as opposed to the Father of lies); Jesus Himself said He was "the truth" and told His disciples to be received "the Spirit of truth". Jesus is the very likeness of all that truth is, who comes from the Father of truth and who gives us His Spirit - the Spirit of truth, so we can like Him. This truth helps us to know right from wrong and truth from error. The Gospel and letters of John highlight this reality more than the other books of the Bible (see: John 1:14; 4:33; 8:42-47; 14:6; 15:26 and 2 John 1:3-4).

In *Unlocking the Bible* (1999), the great theologian - David Pawson (1920-) points out that the Bible and especially the Book of Acts (which we began *this* book talking about) is theologically Trinitarian through and through.

More specifically, it is about:

1. **The kingdom of the Father**
2. **The name of the Son**
3. **The power of the Spirit**

It is Mr. Pawson's desire (and mine too) that each believer understands all three components in their spiritual walk. For they are the key elements necessary in sharing the Gospel. People should be introduced to God as a triune being. When Christ gave the Great Commission, He said to baptise people in the name of the Father, the Son and the Holy Spirit, i.e. to introduce them to the three persons of the Godhead (Matt. 28:19).

So, in closing this chapter, let me unpack those three elements of Trinitarian faith:

1. **We conceive <u>the Kingdom of God the Father</u>** within us when we turn away from our sins - recognising our need for God and His love, mercy and forgiveness in our lives.

2. **We believe in <u>the name of His Son Jesus</u>,** namely that He is the Lord (not ourselves) and that He died and rose again to save us from our sins and to offer us eternal life.

3. **We receive <u>the power of His Holy Spirit</u>** as a result of repentance and belief. As a public and personal symbol of our salvation in God, we get baptised in water in the name of the Father, Son and Spirit. This recognises their work in the person's regeneration. Some people seem to experience the Spirit's baptism more fully later, but either way, He equips believers with fruit and gifts to live as Christ lived. When Christ returns He will fully

establish His Father's Kingdom on Earth, in which all faithful believers will live forever.

Jesus said, "Anyone who loves me will obey my teaching. My Father will love them, and <u>we will come to them and make our home with them</u>." (John 14:23). The way the Father and the Son make their home in our hearts is by the Spirit, who Jesus said would inhabit all those who received Him (John 14:15-17). He is the Spirit of the Father and the Son (Matt. 10:20, Gal. 4:6).

2.

THE LIFE OF CHRIST +
THE CHRISTIAN IN THE SPIRIT

"When the Advocate comes,
whom I will send to you from the Father
- the Spirit of truth who goes out from the
Father
- he will testify about me."

John 15:26

Christ called us to follow Him, and if we are to learn more about the Holy Spirit and His relevance to us as followers of 'the Way', let us study Christ's relationship with the Holy Spirit. After all, Jesus Christ set the ultimate example of how to live the Christian life and was Himself led by the Holy Spirit in all He said and did. He was filled with the Holy Spirit.

The Apostle John shows us "how we know we are in him: whoever claims to live in him must live as Jesus did." (1 John 2:9). So, in order to live as Jesus lived, we must have His Spirit helping us and living inside of us.

In Luke 3, we read of Jesus' baptism in the Jordon River:

Now when all the people were baptized, and when Jesus also had been baptized and was praying, the heavens were opened, and the Holy Spirit descended on him in bodily form, like a dove; and a voice came from heaven, "You are my beloved Son; with you I am well pleased."

Luke 3:21-22 (see also: John 1:32-34)

There are three main things to note:

- Jesus was baptised in water and in the Spirit as well
- We see the Father, Son and Spirit together
- God the Father approves of His Son Jesus before He had even started His ministry! Jesus Himself said elsewhere that the Father had put His "seal of approval" on Him (John 6:27).

As followers of Jesus, saved and sanctified by His death on the cross, we come from that place of approval and sanctification in God. We do not do things to earn God's favour – He already approves when we repent and follow Him, for only faith pleases Him (John 6:28-9, Heb. 11:3). Faith in thought, word and deed is the only thing required. The world on the other hand does things to gain approval. They have it the wrong way around. Film stars, soap stars, music artists and models are forever doing weird and wacky things to get our attention and often live completely messed-up lives leading to 'rehab'.

In spite of this, most young people look up to them as their idols, their inspiration, their role models and to help them form their own identity, beliefs and behaviour. I firmly believe that it is up to us to let the young know that Jesus is their only completely good, balanced, reliable role model, who was totally led by the pure and truthful <u>Holy</u> Spirit of God.

Going from His baptism in Luke 3 into Luke 4, we read that Jesus was led into the desert by the Spirit and spent 40 days there, where He was tempted by the Devil. Afterwards, He began His three-year ministry on Earth. If we study Luke 4, we see that there are four key aspects to learn about Jesus' relationship with the Spirit of God:

- He was filled with the Spirit (vs. 1)
- He was led by the Spirit (vs. 1)
- He went in the power of the Spirit (vs. 14, 36)
- He Himself says that the Spirit of the Lord was upon Him (vs. 18)

So, Jesus did not work in His own power, but by the power of God through the Spirit that was within Him (John 12:49, Acts 1:2, Rom. 8:11). Likewise, we also must act under the guidance of the Holy Spirit if we are to live as Christ lived and fulfil the ministerial call that the Father has placed on our lives. Since the resurrection, Jesus communicated to His disciples through His Spirit (John 20:22, Acts 1:2). The same is true today.

Back in Luke 4, when Jesus was led by the Spirit into the desert to pray, fast and where He was tempted, notice that each of Satan's temptations start out with the phrase, "<u>If</u> you are the Son of God..." or, "<u>If</u> you worship me" (see: Luke 4:3, 7 and 9). You see, just some days earlier, the Father had just spoken a powerful truth over Jesus saying, "You are <u>My beloved Son</u>; in You I am well pleased" and the Spirit came down to confirm this. The role and work of the Spirit here provide a partial foundation for the sacrament of 'Holy Confirmation' in church, which relates to the Spirit's seal of approval on us.

In the situation in the desert, the Devil was already attacking Christ's identity, assuredness and sonship. He asserts that if indeed Jesus is the Son of God He has supernatural power and therefore, He so should use it to feed His starved body. He's tempting Jesus to give into the flesh with the power given to Him from His Father.

After all, He could turn the stones scattered on the desert floor into pieces of bread. But Jesus' responds with the words: "Man shall not live by bread alone, but by <u>every word of God</u>", which is a partial quote of Deuteronomy 8:3. The full verse ends with, "that proceeds from the mouth of God", which is a reference to the <u>breath of God</u>. In other words, Jesus is saying, 'I rely on the Word and the Spirit for my nourishment and not just on physical food and fleshly concerns'. After all, Jesus went 40 days without physical nourishment. He needed to strengthen His spirit to carry out the work His Father had called Him to do.

Jesus is setting an example here. He's showing us that spiritual things weigh much more than physical, carnal things (see: 1 Tim. 4:8). He's also showing us that when we are tempted by the enemy (and we will be), we should not argue or give in, but should just use the Word against him.

The Apostle Peter once said,

Be well balanced (temperate, sober of mind), be vigilant *and* cautious <u>at all times</u>; for that enemy of yours, the devil, roams around like a lion roaring [in fierce hunger], seeking someone to seize upon *and* devour. Withstand him; be firm in faith [against <u>his onset</u>—rooted, established, strong, immovable, and determined], knowing that the same (identical) sufferings are appointed to your brotherhood (the whole body of Christians) throughout the world.

1 Peter 5:8-9
(Words in brackets and italics are found in the
Amplified Classic Version of the Bible)

Our Identity in Christ

We are a body, soul and spirit and yet we often put more emphasis on our bodies and our flesh, which will not last beyond the grave (2 Cor. 5:1-10). Our soul and spirit will live forever, so we should focus more on those parts of our being than on the former (1 Cor 5:5, Rev. 20:4).

Jesus said that life was worth more than clothing, food and drink (Matt. 6:19-34) and Paul says to set our minds on higher, heavenly things (Col. 3:2) because the Spirit and flesh are at war with each other and to win the battle we must be continually led and filled by the Spirit (see: Rom. 7-8, Gal. 5). Clothes, food, the internet, music, football (or footBaal as someone once called it) are nothing compared to knowing Christ and being filled by his wonderful, exciting Holy Spirit who leads us to places we would never have been without Him.

The Devil attacks our identity in God in the same way that He attacked Christ's. Jesus quoted the scriptures back to the Devil instead of arguing with Him, which is what we must do. One of the weapons that God gives us against the enemy is "the sword of the Spirit, which is the Word of God" (Eph. 6:10-18). The word 'sword' is just 'word' with an 's' at the front – which for us can stand for 'Spirit'. Again it shows how the Word and the Spirit work together in us so we grow closer to our Heavenly Father.

It is the Spirit in us who assures us of our identity and who we are in Christ:

> If anyone does not have the Spirit of Christ, they do not belong to Christ…if you live according to the flesh, you will die; but if by the Spirit you put to death the misdeeds of the body, you will live. For those who are led by the Spirit of God are the children of God. The Spirit you received does not make you slaves, so that you live in fear again; rather, the Spirit you received brought about your adoption to sonship. And by him we cry, 'Abba, Father.' The Spirit himself testifies with our spirit that we are God's children. Now if we are children, then we are heirs — heirs of God and co-heirs with Christ, if indeed we share in his sufferings in order that we may also share in his glory.

Romans 8:9b, 13-17 (see also: Mark 14:36)

There again, we read how God as Father, Son and Spirit should be allowed to work in every believer. We must know God as He really is.

When Jesus returned from the desert "full of the Spirit" He was rejected (Luke 4:28-30) and not too long after was scoffed at by people saying He was *just* "the son of a carpenter" (Matt. 13:53-58). So, both the Devil and man were questioning His sonship. Jesus continued on regardless, confident in God alone who assured Him through the Spirit. God wants to do the same for us when we are attacked by the world and the Devil.

In Acts 15:8-9, Peter speaks on how God accepts us irrespective of our background and it is in the giving of His Holy Spirit who confirms this in us. We might not come from a privileged background or have a parent who's a lawyer, a professor or a chief executive, but that doesn't matter if we know the affirmation and love of our Father through the Spirit and through the studying of the Word. Our identity is in God alone, though Christ, whose Spirit leads us to being more holy.

The Gospel

Jesus commanded His disciples to spread the Gospel from Jerusalem to the ends of the Earth, but not to leave Jerusalem until the Holy Spirit had come and empowered them for the task (Acts 1:4-8).

The spread of the Gospel in the Spirit is like the 'ripple effect' caused by dropping a stone in a pool of water or tapping your foot on its surface. I remember one windy day in my local park where I randomly tapped my foot on the surface of a slow-moving stream. I watched as the ripples spread further and further out, but then weakened and flattened as they grew. Rocks sticking over the surface broke the ripple early, but when the wind was blowing in the same general direction as that ripple, I noticed it caused it to go further and can even push water over rocks and much further than it could have gone on its own. Wind also creates an impression on the water which adds more ripples.

Jesus said that those who were born of the Spirit were like the wind which blows here and there (John 3:8). A wind filled the place where the believers were when the power of the Spirit fell on them - completing their new birth in Christ (Acts 2:2). You achieve so much more when led and filled by the Spirit. The word for 'wind' in Hebrew is 'ruach' which means 'spirit'. The word 'spirit' is also where we get the word 'inspire' — as it means to be 'spirited'.

Not by [man's] might, nor by [man's] power, but by my Spirit says the Lord.

Zechariah 4:6 (see also: Isa. 30:1)

The Spirit of Christ in us

The Holy Spirit does everything Jesus did, therefore as the Bible says (Rom. 8:9, 16) we cannot be like Jesus without His Holy Spirit communing with our spirit:

Jesus went in the power of the Spirit – who is the Spirit of Jesus.	Luke 4, Acts 16:7
Jesus stood strong against Satan with the Word and full of the Spirit – the Word of God is the Sword of the Spirit and a weapon against Satan, and also the Spirit of truth reminds of the truth of God's Word.	Matt 4.1-13; 16:13, Eph. 6:10-18
Jesus only said and did what the Father told Him and Jesus said the Spirit would be the same.	John 16:12-15
Jesus healed people – the Holy Spirit heals us.	Luke 4:14-41, Acts 10:38, 1 Cor. 12:9
Jesus brought us joy and in His Spirit and Presence is fullness of joy.	Ps. 16:11, John 14:27
Jesus lifts our burden and helps us when we're heavy laden – the Holy Spirit strengthens us in our weakness and removes our fears.	Matt. 11:28-30, Acts 4:31, Rom. 8:26, 2 Tim. 1:7
Jesus helped, comforted, counselled and is our Advocate and said the Holy Spirit would be our Helper, Comforter, Counsellor and Advocate.	Is. 9:6, Matt. 5:4, John 14:16; 26; 1 John 2:1,

Jesus' sacrifice on the cross tore the diving curtain in the temple between us and God and the Holy Spirit fills our bodies and helps to heal out torn lives which are now the temple of His Spirit / God's holy Presence.	Matt. 27:51, 1 Cor. 6.19-20
Jesus was raised from the dead in the power of the Holy Spirit, who now also lives in us.	Rom. 1:4; 8:11, Eph. 3:16-17, 2 Tim. 1:6-7
Jesus commanded us to spread the Gospel, and it is only by the Holy Spirit that this is accomplished.	Matt. 28:19, 1 Cor. 2:4, 1 Pet. 1:10-12
Jesus valued us and assured us that He'd always be with us and the Holy Spirit is that deposited assurance of our place in Him and His presence.	Matt. 28:20, Rom. 8:9, 16; 1 Cor. 1:21-22, 1 Thes. 1:4-7
Jesus intercedes for us and so does the Holy Spirit.	Rom. 8:34, 26

If you are feeling burdened and sapped of energy then ask God to fill you more with His Spirit - He can give such a lightness to your body, soul and spirit. Remember, that God does things in His timing. Ask Him to show any unholy areas in your life that may be weighing you down and blocking more of His Holy Spirit from entering.

Where the Spirit of the Lord there is freedom.

2 Corinthians 3:17

The author of *Tortured for Christ* and *Alone for God*, Richard Wurmbrand (1909-2001), was a Romanian minister who was imprisoned for publicly stating that communism and Christianity were incompatible. He was placed in solitary confinement for 14 years, but said that the internal freedom he enjoyed in God exceeded the external confinement he endured in prison. His spiritual life was more important than the physical. He had the Holy Spirit living within in Him - that same Spirit who liberates the captives (Isa. 61). As Wurmbrand put it:

> Real freedom does not depend upon external circumstances. There exists the wonderful liberty of which the children of God partake, even when in straitened circumstances or trammelled by prison walls.

> (Wurmbrand, 1988)

I love the verse in the Old Testamanet where Samuel anoints Saul with oil and prophesies that the Spirit would come upon, saying that when that happens **"you will be changed into a different person."** We read that soon after the people around Saul were amazed at how spiritual and prophetic Saul had become (see: 1 Sam. 10:6-11). How true that is for anyone who is filled by God's Holy Spirit. However, we must follow His lead, as sadly, Saul did not and changed into an insecure, self-absorbed individual. The Spirit of God left him, and this made him vulnerable to an evil spirit that God allowed to affect him (see: 1 Sam. 16).

I remember in a previous church I attended, there was a great sermon about the gifts of the Spirit one Sunday. The pastor speaking told of an extremely timid woman who once came to him and his wife about her timidity. They prayed over her to receive more of the Holy Spirit. She went to work the next day and her colleagues were overwhelmed by the dramatic change in her character and behaviour. The Lord had removed that excessive fear and replaced it with faith and confidence in Him.

> For the Spirit God gave us does not make us timid, but gives us power, love and self-discipline.
>
> 2 Timothy 1:7

The New King James Version says, "For God has not given us a spirit of fear, but of power and of love and of a sound mind." Remember what the three people Dorothy meets in *The Wizard of Oz* (1939) wanted from the Wizard?

- the Lion wanted the power of courage to overcome his cowardly fear
- the Tinman wanted a heart so he could love
- the Scarecrow wanted a brain so he could think soundly in his mind.

Thankfully God is not like the Wizard who was pompous, corrupt and demanding and had to apologise in the end. God is only too willing to give you His Holy Spirit if you repent and receive Him gladly.

Why not ask for the gifts of the Spirit that He wants you to use and develop? You can find out what role He wants you to take and this will lead to you being so much more joyful, fulfilled and effective in God's Kingdom.

People usually get baptised in the Spirit by the physical laying on of hands (Acts 8:17; 19:6; 1 Tim. 4:14; 2 Tim. 1:6), so ask someone who you trust is God-fearing, Word-focused and Spirit-led to pray over you for more of God's Holy Spirit! God will direct you to the right people if you wholeheartedly place your confidence in Him. If you struggle to trust Him, tell Him. He knows anyway, but He wants to commune with you (Matt. 6:8).

A lot of people feel uncomfortable with receiving the Spirit's baptism because they wonder how a physical act can have a spiritual effect. In the western world, and especially in the UK, our minds and hearts (even if we are Christian) have been heavily influenced by Greek philosophy - from democracy to our economics to the Olympics and the love of sport to even the pantheon-like designs of London's fiscal buildings and much of its public art - Grecian ways have become our ways.

The Greeks separated the physical from the spiritual, and either lived for self-indulgence or in an over-the-top lofty, spiritual way. But the Hebrew thinking was to combine the physical and the spiritual. Our God is Spirit and yet made the physical world (see: the Genesis 1 / John 1 comparison in chapter 1). Adam and Eve physically ate the forbidden fruit, which had a profoundly spiritual effect on the whole world. Christ's physical death spiritually saves anyone who believes - they receive His Spirit and this enlivens their spirit.

Praying in the Spirit

Our Lord Jesus had a powerful prayer life, but He did it all through the Spirit. In the scriptures, there are several calls for Christians to continually "pray in the Spirit". Paul in particular, emphasises it in his famous eighth chapter of Romans; and in Ephesians 6, he states that it as one of the weapons that a believer can use in their constant fight against the enemy.

Why do we need to pray in the Spirit?

Just hours before His arrest in the Garden of Gethsemane, when He was in one of the darkest and loneliest moments of His life, Jesus expressed real upset that His disciples failed to stay awake and pray with Him when He needed it most. He woke them up and told Peter: "Watch and pray that you may not enter into temptation. The spirit indeed is willing, but the flesh is weak." (Matt. 26:14).

God has made us to be a body a soul and a spirit. We are a tri-part being, just as He is, because we are made in His image. When we come to faith in Christ, our spirit (which was once dead to God) is made alive by His Spirit coming into us, who "testifies with our spirit" that we are now His (Rom. 8:16, Eph. 2). Before we knew Christ, we mainly served the flesh - the soulish / body part of our being - we sought worldly things first, but now we "do not live according to the flesh but according to the Spirit." (Rom. 8:4) so we seek more spiritual things.

But even when we are with Christ (as the disciples were), we still struggle against the more carnal / fleshly desires of the past. In Gethsemane against such utter temptation, Christ was reminding His disciples that even though their spirit may be in communion with him, their flesh was still weak and gives into temptation far too easily. Therefore, considering that the Holy Spirit testifies with our spirit and Christ Himself called us to be led by the Spirit (John 14-16), we need to "pray in the Spirit". This means we are led by the Spirit in our prayers, so we know what to pray and how to pray to overcome the weaknesses of the flesh.

Our prayer life will radically transform our whole life and through it we will find it easier to overcome certain temptations that once tormented us in the past. Christ "who was tempted in every way we are" will provide a way out through His sufficient grace towards us in the Holy Spirit (1 Cor. 10:13, 2 Cor. 12:9). We must get more in touch with His Spirit.

For as Paul says,

> ...the Spirit helps us in our weakness. We do not know what we ought to pray for, but the Spirit himself intercedes for us through wordless groans. And he who searches our hearts knows the mind of the Spirit, because the Spirit intercedes for God's people in accordance with the will of God.

> Romans 8:26-27

Apart from in times of crisis, prayer can actually be an unnatural and difficult thing to do. As Paul says, "[we] do not know what we ought to pray", yet the Spirit guides us if we regularly ask and trust Him to. He prays through us, so that we are praying by our spirit, and not from a selfish/soulish/fleshly place.

The disciples asked Jesus how to pray and He told them to address their Father and to pray in His name - in the name of Jesus (Matt. 6:5-15, John 15:16; 16:23, see also: Eph. 5:20). He said not to repeat prayers over and over again as that becomes meaningless. It is the Spirit's role to help our prayers to be fresh, relevant and helpful:

- we pray to our Father in Heaven
- with Christ's Name to sign it
- and the Spirit helps us pray the right prayers in the first place.

How much more help could we ask for?

We invoke the three persons of the Trinity as God is one and from the New Testament onwards God has been revealed to us in this way - three in one and one in three.

Jesus Himself prayed to the Father (Matt. 11:25-26, Luke 23:24, John 11:41-42; 17, Heb. 5:7), He was the Son (Matt. 26:63-64, Luke 1:35, John 1:14) was led by the Spirit in all matters, including prayer (Matt. 12:28, Luke 4:1, Acts 10:38). This does not mean we cannot speak to Christ or to the Spirit in our prayer times, for Stephen called on Jesus to receive Him upon his death (Acts 7:59), we are told to "call on the name of Jesus" and to have fellowship with Him (1 Cor. 1:2-9). John describes how he, the church and the Spirit say, "Come Lord Jesus" (Rev. 22:20).

When we 'pray in the Spirit', we acknowledge the Spirit in our prayers (Rom. 8:26, Eph. 6:18, Jude 0:20). After all, He is the voice of the Father and Son (Matt. 10:20, John 12:32, Heb. 3:7-8; 10:15-18). We are encouraged to respond to His voice, which can surely include responding in prayer. In 2 Timothy 1:14, Paul says to protect the truth of the Gospel in us "with the help of the Holy Spirit who lives in us."

In Acts 8:26-40, we read of when the Apostle Philip responded to the Spirit's call by sharing the Gospel to a rich Ethiopian eunuch, who accepted it gladly. I've heard that the eunuch headed back to ancient Ethiopia with the Gospel message, bringing salvation to thousands there and the millions living across the African continent. Look what happens when we respond to the Spirit's call. His wind blows on the ripple of the Word and it spreads out far and wide as we are obedient. And in Philip's case, he literally was blow by the wind of the Spirit (Acts 8:39-40)!

This event along with countess others also helped fulfil Jesus' words to His disciples (including Philip) that they would be empowered by the Spirit and that this would enable the Gospel message to go from Jerusalem and unto the ends of the Earth (Acts 1:8). Indeed, Ethiopia seemed as though it was at the ends of the Earth to those living in the Holy Land at that time.

Jesus commanded His followers to baptise new disciples in the name of the Father, the Son and the Spirit. This tells me that as part of that baptismal prayer, we are surely calling on the Spirit and therefore acknowledging Him verbally (Matt. 28:19-20). More specially, we are acknowledging Him personally (and equally alongside the Father and the Son) and asking Him by His power to cleanse the person we are baptising and to anoint them to become a disciple. We are communicating with Him, and so yes, I believe we can call on the Spirit personally.

Even so, there is very little emphasis on praying to the Spirit and indeed, the general Biblical pattern in prayer is to pray:

> **to : the Father**
> **by : the Son**
> **in : the Spirit**

In his letter, Jude warns against people "who divide [the church], who follow mere natural instincts and do not have the Spirit." He continues: "But you, dear friends...[build] yourselves up in your most holy faith and [by] praying in the Holy Spirit." (Jude 0:19-20). But what does he mean? The Greek words for 'pray in' ('proseuchomenoi' and 'en') can mean 'with the help of' and 'in the sphere of'.

This relates to Paul's words in Romans 8:26 about the Spirit helping us in our weaknesses and in the times when we simply do not how what to pray. Praying in the Spirit can also refer to praying in tongues (see: 1 Corinthians 14).

So why not ask the Holy Spirit of God to inspire and influence your prayer life so that your prayers are more effective and more in keeping with the Father's will and so you draw closer to Jesus!

3.

THE FRUIT OF THE SPIRIT

"Spirit of the living God, fall afresh on us.
Spirit of the living God, fall afresh on us.
Melt us, mold us, fill us, use me,
Spirit of the living God, fall afresh on us."

Paul Armstrong, 1984

I firmly believe that when we come to Christ, His Spirit comes to live in us and we receive 'the fruit of the Spirit' in seed form. In Matthew 7, Jesus used the imagery of a fruit tree to represent a person. He explains that false believers in God are like diseased fruit trees who only produce bad fruits (bad behaviours), but true believers are like healthy trees who produce good fruit (good behaviours). He says, "you will recognize them by their fruits." (see: Matt. 7:15-20). So, it's about discerning if someone is genuine or not by what they do or don't do for the Lord.

Later on, in Matthew's Gospel, we read of when Jesus curses a fig tree because it only sprouted leaves, but no fruit (see: Matt. 21:18-21). From a distance it looked to Jesus like a proper fig tree, which is supposed to grow leaves and fruit together.

As Christians, we should not pretend to be like others, and look full of life, but be fruitless. We have to bear Godly fruit as well, which are the results of our continued faith in God, our Godly words, thoughts and actions. For "faith by itself, if it is not accompanied by action, is dead" (see: Jas. 2:14-26). To this day a person will say "I can see the fruits of my labour" or say that someone's behaviour was like "sour grapes".

In John's Gospel, Jesus said:

I am the vine; you are the branches. If you remain in me and I in you, you will bear much fruit; apart from me you can do nothing.

John 15:5 (see also: Jude 0:11-13)

So more specifically, what is this fruit and how do we show godly fruit?

Paul elaborates on spiritual fruit in his letter to the Galatians. According to him, it is the Spirit who enables us to show godly fruit. It cannot be produced by moral discipline alone. So, in order to bear much fruit and remain on the vine we must be led by the Spirit. He will show us how to achieve what Christ asked. He describes the types of fruit those who are ungodly will show and the types of fruit those who are in Christ will show:

76

...I say, walk by the Spirit, and you will not gratify the desires of the flesh. For the desires of the flesh are against the Spirit, and the desires of the Spirit are against the flesh, for these are opposed to each other, to keep you from doing the things you want to do. But if you are led by the Spirit, you are not under the law. Now the works of the flesh are evident: sexual immorality, impurity, sensuality, idolatry, sorcery, enmity, strife, jealousy, fits of anger, rivalries, dissensions, divisions, envy, drunkenness, orgies, and things like these. I warn you, as I warned you before, that those who do such things will not inherit the kingdom of God. But <u>the fruit of the Spirit is love, joy, peace, patience, kindness, goodness, faithfulness, gentleness, self-control</u>...

Galatians 5:16-23
('gentleness' is often translated as either 'meekness' or
'humility')

With the exception of love, many people think of the fruits of the Spirit as just applying to the way we treat others, yet, all nine of them can apply to our relationship with God and even with ourselves. So, just as we are called to love God and love our neighbour as we love ourselves, we should ask ourselves - do we have peace with God, with others and with ourselves? We may display patience with others, but are we patient with God and with ourselves? Do we wait on Him and give ourselves enough room or are we undisciplined and so give ourselves too much attention? Are we too hard on ourselves or with others or even with God? It is the

Spirit's role to ripen good fruit in us to affect all our relationships, as we surrender to Him.

Notice above how Paul doesn't speak of "the fruits of the Spirit", but rather the "fruit of the Spirit" (singular). This is because we must show all the fruit and not just some of them. It is like one fruit which is available in many varieties and kinds. The first fruit or variety of the overall fruit is 'love'. It is no surprise that Paul lists it first, for Paul says that love is the greatest virtue of all (1 Cor. 13:13) Jesus made is clear that the greatest commandments that are must follow are all about love (Matt. 22:36-40).

When we show love to God, our neighbour and ourselves, the other eight fall into place, because it is from a seedbed of love that they grow from. For example, without love you cannot be patient, kind or humble, because as Paul tells us "Love is patient, love is kind. It does not envy, it does not boast, it is not proud..." and "without love" we are "only a resounding gong or a clanging cymbal" - it is just lip-service or hot air without love (see: 1 Cor. 13).

God's kindness is often referred to as His "lovingkindness" in many Bible translations (Psa. 36:7; Isa. 63:4; Tis. 3:4). It is one of my favourite words to describe God.

After listing the fruit(s) of the Spirit above, Paul makes this statement:

> Against such things there is no law.
>
> Galatians 5:23

In other words, no one can say that those qualities are wrong. You cannot or should not try to legislate against those qualities. No one should block another from showing them.

At the outset of this message Paul said to "walk in the Spirit", and at the end he states:

> ...Since we live by the Spirit, <u>let us keep in step with the Spirit</u>.
>
> Galatians 5:24-25.

How do I live in the Spirit and keep in step with Him?

Firstly, study how Christ behaved - He is our example and He lived entirely by the Spirit. We cannot be perfect like Him in this life, but as we learn about how He lived we will know the right ways of living. It is the Spirit's role to strengthen us to be like Christ and more we allow Him to - the harder we will find it to sin.

Some pointers about Christ:

- Jesus sought time with the Father every day regardless of circumstances (Matt. 14:13, Mark 1:35, Mark 6:45-46, Mark 14:32-34, Luke 4:42, Luke 5:16, Luke 6:12, Luke 9:18, John 6:15). Even He - the sinless Son of God needed to pray to the Father and maintain a reverent relationship with Him, and therefore as Christ-ians, so must we.

- He taught us to do the same - how to pray, fast, trust and put God first above all other concerns (Matt. 6).

- Jesus regularly went to the synagogue and the Temple and encouraged people to study the Word - as He knew it perfectly (Matt. 9:13, Luke 2:46-47; 4:16-22; 24:45-48, John 1:1-14).

- Jesus said to get to know people by their fruits. He is sharing an insightful way into understanding the genuine believers who can help us in our walk with Him (Matt. 7:15-20). I would also encourage you to always seek help from a trusted Biblically-sound believer and listen to teachings of Biblically-sound teachers. Ask and patiently trust the Lord to direct you to the right people.

The fruit of the Spirit is in fact a description of the character of Christ. He lived by the Spirit and was so loving, joyful, peaceful, patient, kind, good, faithful, gentle and self-controlled (see: table below). Indeed, the prophet Isaiah said that the Messiah would "bear fruit" and that "the Spirit of the Lord shall rest upon him, the Spirit of wisdom and understanding, the Spirit of counsel and might, the

Spirit of knowledge and the fear of the Lord." (see: Isa. 11:1-2).
There are seven spirits mentioned there encompassed by the one
Holy Spirit, hence John's use of the phrase: "the Seven-fold Spirit"
in Revelation, which rested on the Lamb and went out into the
world to all believers (see: Rev. 1:4; 3:1; 4:5-6; 5:6).

So, when you first believed in Christ and were born again in
the Spirit, it would have been like a seed sown in you. As you grow
in Him, those seeds should sprout to produce Christ-like wisdom,
understanding, counsel, might, knowledge and a healthy,
reverential fear of the Lord in you. It is the same principle as with
the fruit of the Spirit.

In regards to the fruit, you can in fact demonstrate all of them
in one just situation. For example, imagine a Christian going to see a
sick friend in hospital. Whilst there, they show:

- **love** by visiting them,
- **joy** by cheering them up,
- **peace** by calming their fears,
- **patience** by listening to the arduous details of their
  operation
- **kindness** by giving them a bunch of grapes,
- **goodness** by offering to look after the children,
- **faithfulness** by praying for them every day,
- **humility** by leaving when the nurse says visiting hours are
  over and
- **self-control** by not eating the grapes.

(Word and Spirit Together, 2009)

It must be said that it is far from easy to demonstrate the fruit of the Spirit, especially all nine forms in one situation. Paul appears to acknowledge this above with his reference to the temptations to give in to fleshly, human desires. We serve a God who forgives us of these things when we confess and repent. His Spirit was sent to gently, but also powerfully show us where we are going wrong and to lovingly help us how to live as Christ lived. As Jesus said, the Holy Spirit would remind us of all He has said and did (John 14:26).

It can be a daily challenge for Christians to keep showing the fruit of the Spirit in a world that is increasingly hostile to Christianity and to "the things of the Spirit" (Rom. 8:5, Gal. 5:17, see also: Jas. 4:4), yet we must not allow our feelings, circumstances or the attacks from outside sources to prevent us from daily living out the fruit of Christ's Spirit. Here are some encouraging words from the Old Testament. Please believe and and allow them to sink in to your spirit:

This is what the Lord says,

'Cursed is the one who trusts in man,
    who draws strength from mere flesh
    and whose heart turns away from the Lord.

That person will be like a bush in the wastelands;
    they will not see prosperity when it comes.
They will dwell in the parched places of the desert,
    in a salt land where no one lives.

'But blessed is the one who trusts in the Lord,
    whose confidence is in him.

They will be like a tree planted by the water
    that sends out its roots by the stream.
It does not fear when heat comes;
    its leaves are always green.
It has no worries in a year of drought
    and never fails to bear fruit.'

The heart is deceitful above all things
    and beyond cure.
    Who can understand it?

'I the Lord search the heart
    and examine the mind,
to reward each person according to their conduct,
    according to what their deeds deserve.'

Jeremiah 17:5-10

Through His eternal Spirit dwelling inside every believer, Jesus can rid the natural inner conflict - the civil war which rages in the heart of every man, woman and child. It is a result of us inheriting that tendency to sin and rebel. The war began in our very first parents - Adam and Eve (Gen. 3, Rom. 5-8). We do not teach children to be naughty or to lie - they instinctively just do it. Despite the wonder and innocence of children, they often learn to say the word 'no' before 'yes'. The Bible says that the "inclination of the human heart is evil from childhood" (Gen. 8:21), but also that

"Out of the mouth of infants and nursing babies you have prepared praise?" (Psa. 8:2, Matt. 21:16).

The conflict is there from childhood, which is why we must come to salvation in Christ. Those of us who know Christ must tell others about the salvation He brings and introduce them to God as Father who wants them to come home, God as the Son who died to save them from their sins and God as Spirit who can live in them filling them with love, joy, peace and much, much more (Matt. 28:19-20). After all, are not all people wanting to be loved? Don't people desire joy and happiness in their personal lives, and peace in the country they live?

One of the ways of spreading the truth of God's Gospel is achieved through the way we treat people. Non-believers should see something in us that they are missing. They should see the fruit of the Spirit coming forth, even if they do not know what they are. Jesus said that it would be through love that all people would know we are His disciples and said that if we love Him, we would love others (John 13:34-35; 14:15-21).

He said the Spirit whom the world cannot accept would help us to love others and keep His commands (rather than trying to do so in the flesh). In union with that Peter (who heard the words of Jesus first hand) said we must revere Christ and His Word above all else and from that place of reverence we should "be prepared to give an answer to everyone who asks [us] to give the reason for the hope that [we] have. But [to] do this with gentleness and respect" (1 Pet. 3:15).

I say with confidence that the nine aspects of the fruit are all qualities most people in this world have and admire in others. The Spirit brings these qualities alive and gives them much more meaning and purpose. The Bible is the best guide in teaching us how to grow and show those fruits for the benefit of others, ourselves and to give glory and honour to God. Only by His Spirit can we grow and show that fruit to its greatest potential. Without Christ we can do nothing that will last forever (John 15:5).

> ... now being made free from sin, and become servants
> to God, you have your fruit unto holiness, and the end
> everlasting life.

> Romans 6:22

The Fruit of the Spirit throughout the Word

All nine varieties of the Spirit's fruit can be found throughout the Bible. God has those qualities and calls all His followers to emulate Him:

QUALITY OF GOD	QUALITY FOR CHRISTIANS
LOVE	
Jer. 31:3, John 3:16; 13:34–35; 1 John 4:10	Lev. 19:18, Deut. 6:4, Matt. 5:43–45; 22:36–40; Rom. 15:30; 1 John 4:8
JOY	
Zeph. 3:17; Luke 15:7	Psalm 16:11; Psa. 33:11, John 10:10, 1 Thes. 1:6
PEACE	
Psa. 29:11, John 14:27; 1 Cor. 14:33	Prov. 12:20, Rom. 8:6; 12:18, Phil. 4:6–7, Col. 3:15
PATIENCE	
Isa. 30:18, 2 Pet. 3:9	2 Cor. 3:12–13, Col. 1:6, 10–12
KINDNESS	
Psa. 63:3, Rom. 2:4; 11:22	Job 6:14, Zec. 7:9; Eph. 4:30–32
GOODNESS	
Exod. 33:19, Psa. 100:5, Acts 10:38	Psa. 23:6, Eph. 5:8–11
FAITHFULNESS	
Psa. 33:4, 1 Cor. 10:13	Ezek. 18:5,9, Luke 16:10; Rev. 2:10
GENTLENESS (HUMILITY, MEEKNESS)	
Psa. 18:35, Matt. 11:29	Prov. 15:1, Phil. 4:5, Jas. 4:6
SELF-CONTROL	
Psa. 30:5; 103:8;	Prov. 21:23, Tis. 2:11–12,

Heb. 4:15	Jas. 1:19-20

There are other lists of godly virtues listed in scripture which are paramount for all believers:

- The Beatitudes, where Jesus commends the meek and the peacemakers - which are two qualities of the fruit of the Spirit (Matt: 5:3-12).

- Paul tells the Corinthians of how he has remained faithful through all circumstances as an example to them. He mentions the Holy Spirit being in and amongst all that (2 Cor. 6:3-10).

- Paul tells the Ephesians to be completely humble, gentle, patient, peaceful and good (five of the nine fruits), which is all part of the kingdom of light and produces "fruit of the light" (Eph. 4:2-3; 5:8-19).

- Paul tells the Philippians to rejoice always and be gentle to all (two of the fruits); to monitor their thinking by dwelling on good things, including what is "lovely" - which refers to the first and most important quality of the Spirit - 'love' (Phil. 4:4-9).

- Paul tells the Colossians to be clothed in "compassion, kindness, humility, gentleness and patience...love...[and] peace", which are seven of the fruits (Col. 3:12-15).

- Paul encourages Timothy to fan the flame of the Spirit's gifts within him by bolding using them, "for God gave us a spirit not of fear but of power and love and self-control." (2 Tim. 1:7). Notice how he refers to the first and last fruits of the Spirit - love and self-control. They are the bookends, which hold the others together. Everything must be done in love and also in a balanced, orderly, wise way.

- James states: "the wisdom from above is first pure, then peaceable, gentle, open to reason, full of mercy and good fruits, impartial and sincere. And a harvest of righteousness is sown in peace by those who make peace." (Jas. 3:17-18). James mentions peace three times, along with a reference to gentility. James identifies that Heavenly wisdom is the best mindset for the growth of "good fruit" in the believer's life.

- Peter says, "Finally, all of you, be like-minded, be sympathetic, love one another, be compassionate and humble." (1 Pet. 3:8). Love and humility are mentioned there, which are two of the fruits (as gentleness is often translated as humility). We must come from a place of humility in order to position ourselves to receive from the Lord (see also: Jas. 4:4-10).

From Fruit to Gifts

I believe that when we first come to Christ and surrender to Him, we are born again, for Jesus refers to this also as being "born of the Spirit" (see: John 3:3-8). His Spirit comes to dwell inside to convict us of sin. This happens more as we grow accustomed to His promptings and come to know His ways through regular study of His Word. We begin to show godly fruit as we allow the seeds of that fruit to grow inside of us. But there's more to walking in the Spirit than just growing and showing godly fruit.

Now as I said, Jesus had all those qualities - He showed all that spiritual fruit, yet He also went around healing the sick. The power to heal is a gift of the Spirit and not a fruit of the Spirit. We can receive that gift along with many others when are "baptised in the Spirit" as Jesus commanded His disciples to be. They could heal even before the Holy Spirit was poured out in that 'baptism of fire', because Jesus was with them. He gave them that power. But He said He had to go away in order for the Holy Spirit to come (John 16:7). Why? Because whilst He was in His human body, He was restricted to where He could be. Whereas His Spirit can go anywhere anytime.

As David Pawson states: "If Jesus was still here on Earth, how often could you receive him at a meeting in your church?" (David Pawson - Charismatics and Evangelicals, 2016). But we can have His Spirit *of* Jesus with us in all situations (Phil. 1:19-20; 1 Pet. 1:8-12).

4.

THE BAPTISM OF THE SPIRIT

**"I baptize you with water,
but he will baptize you with the Holy Spirit."**

Mark 1:8

As a public declaration of our new faith in Christ and as a symbol of being spiritual cleansed - we get baptised in water, yet, many Christians do not experience the baptism of the Holy Spirit - otherwise known as 'the baptism of fire'. This is usually because they have not been taught about it or have even been taught against it. Some are baptized in the Spirit at new birth, yet do not realise it, again because they haven't been taught about Him.

The group of Ephesian believers in Acts 19 had not heard about it, so if you are like them, you are not alone. Let me explore this and try to persuade you of the importance of the Spirit's baptism for you and your walk with Jesus.

The promise of the empowering Spirit

When God breathed into Adam, He gave Him life (Gen. 2:7). Jesus said that just as we are all born physically as flesh, we must also be born "of the Spirit" (John 3:3-16). I believe the 'born again' experience may well have been experienced by the disciples when Jesus:

> **...breathed on them and said, 'Receive the Holy Spirit.'**
>
> John 20:22

Here, Jesus is demonstrating to His Disciples what would happen to them on Pentecost Sunday – that the Spirit would breathe down on them from Heaven. Therefore, He's commanding them to be receptive of the Spirit. As promised, He is not leaving them as orphans without spiritual help, for earlier He said to them, "I will come to you" and also that the Spirit "will be in you" (see: John 14:16-18). In other words, 'I will come to you in the form of the Holy Spirit'.

Before His death, Jesus had told them that the Spirit which currently dwelt "with" them would soon come "in" to them (see: John 14:17). He also said He'd ask the Father to send the Spirit, but that this would not happen until He had left the Earth.

In all this, we see the roles of the three persons of the Godhead:

- The Father promises and sends the baptism of the Spirit (Luke 24:49, John 14:16)
- the Son is the baptiser and He Himself lived a life baptised in the Spirit as an example to us (Mark 1:8, 12, Acts 10:38)
- The Spirit is the one who a believer is baptised in (Acts 2:4, 1 Cor. 12:3)

Jesus later goes onto say,

"…wait for the gift my Father promised, which you have heard me speak about. For John baptised with water, but in a few days <u>you will be baptised with the Holy Spirit…you will receive power when the Holy Spirit comes on you</u>"

(Acts 1:4, see also: Acts 11:16).

The Greek word for 'power' is 'dunamis', which is where we get the word 'dynamite' from! So, Jesus promised the disciples an explosive fire that would remove fear and doubt and give them a grace, an authority and a confidence to spread the truth in the face of fear and persecution. They would become dynamite disciples!

We should surely ask ourselves, when we evangelise, are we convincing people of the truth of the Gospel in an intellectual way and just preaching <u>at</u> people *or* are people being touched by a grace, power authority and confidence that they see in us? Do they notice something different about us that they know they want and need?

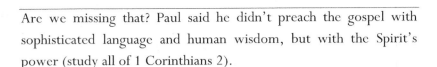
Are we missing that? Paul said he didn't preach the gospel with sophisticated language and human wisdom, but with the Spirit's power (study all of 1 Corinthians 2).

You see, Jesus told the disciples that they must be "clothed with power from on high" and Paul tells us not to follow the ways of the flesh, but to be baptised "into Christ" and to "clothe yourselves with Christ" (see: Luke 24:49, Rom. 13:14, Gal. 3:27). Just as certain colours and certain clothes do not suit certain people, so too - certain behaviours in Christians do not look good and are *not* good. We must be clothed and immersed in Him in order to change the evil ways within. We are changed from the inside out. Indeed, the word 'baptism' and 'baptise' come from the Greek 'baptizo', which means to be "immersed" or "clothed".

You are probably familiar with water baptism, but as Jesus said, there is a second baptism that all His followers should experience:

> For John baptised with water, but in a few days you
> will be baptised with the Holy Spirit.'
>
> > Acts 1:5
>
> The word 'with' here can mean 'in' as well.

If Jesus went through both water and fire baptism, so should all those who follow Him. After all, He said to Nicodemus that a person must be "born of water and the Spirit" (John 3:5). John the Baptist spoke of this too, for he said:

I baptize you with water for repentance, but he who is coming after me is mightier than I... He will baptize you with the Holy Spirit and fire.

Matthew 3:11

When we were baptised in water, it was a sign that we were cleansed from the stains of sin, but that empty, swept-clean self needs filling with something. Yes, the Spirit comes into us when we are born again and some say that is the baptism of the Spirit, yet for many there is no filling up without a further experience. The New Age religion says to 'clear your mind', but the Bible says to fill your mind with the goodness of God (Phil. 4:8), with prayer (1 Pet. 4:7) and to adopt the mind of the Spirit which leads to "life and peace" (Rom. 8:6, 27). Being empty leaves us open to the enemy.

Jesus said:

When an impure spirit comes out of a person, it goes through arid places seeking rest and does not find it. Then it says, 'I will return to the house I left.' When it arrives, it finds the house swept clean and put in order. Then it goes and takes seven other spirits more wicked than itself, and they go in and live there. And the final condition of that person is worse than the first.

Luke 11:24-26

So instead of being open to evil, we often need the infilling of God's Holy Spirit to fill that cleaned out vacuum. Just being purified of sin, impure spirits and other ungodly things by repentance can actually sometimes leave people negative - because they say well I don't smoke, I don't gamble, I don't sleep around anymore...I don't, I don't, I don't... and *they don't* really get to know the wonder and amazingness of being filled more with the Spirit of God. They don't succumb so easily to the pleasure and power of sin anymore, but they also don't fully enjoy the pleasure and power of the Spirit! They are stuck somewhere in the middle. It is like being stuck in between the ascension and Pentecost. Let me reiterate - Jesus made it crystal clear that we must "Receive the Holy Spirit" (John 20:22). Four simple words.

In Psalm 51, David prayed to God "create in me a clean heart...[and] do not take your Holy Spirit from me". He knew it wasn't enough to just be cleaned out or cleansed - he needed an infilling of God's Spirit too. Even though David lived long before the Spirit was poured out "on all flesh" who believed in the Messiah, he and many other holy people who really followed God and looked to the coming of the promised Messiah were given God's Spirit in them or at least to rest upon them for a time.

The Spirit came in power on David, after leaving King Saul - who was then tormented by an evil spirit due to his sin (1 Sam. 16:13-14). So, when we are not filled or at least influenced by God's Spirit and we turn away from God as Saul did, we can be open to an evil spirit or at least some sort of influence from Satan.

The purpose of being baptised in the Spirit's fire is to empower you with spiritual gifts or enhance the ones you already have been using, as I will discuss in the next chapter. Some people get baptized in the Spirit the moment they come to Christ (Acts 2:38, Acts 10:44-46; 11:15-16), but for many it is a separate experience that comes later. For example, in Acts 8:12-17, Peter and John encounter a group of people for whom the Holy Spirit had not yet fully come upon. So, Peter and John laid hands on them to be more immersed in the Holy Spirit. It appears those people had only been taught about Jesus and not about His Spirit. There are many people like that today.

Don't you want more of him in your life, like they did?

We can become miserable saints if we get cleaned out, but don't allow our lives and our souls to be immersed in the Spirit to a greater extent (either through ignorance or resistance). You see, being baptised in water deals with the past, but being baptised in fire deals with the future. Water baptism is like a burial - you are baptised into Christ's death and it represents the death of your old nature (Rom. 6:1-5). Through the baptism in the Spirit, a person becomes equipped with new or enhanced spiritual gifts, which greatly help them fulfil their future calling in Christ (Rom. 1:11).

In Ephesians 4, doesn't Paul say that there is only "one body and one Spirit...one hope...one Lord, one faith, <u>one baptism</u>, one God and Father..."

Yes, but there, Paul is speaking of the water baptism as an outward act where one professes their "one faith" in their "one Lord". Paul then mentions the "one Spirit" needed in a person's life, which is surely a reference to being baptised or filled with the Spirit anyway. He also speaks later in Ephesians 4 of the Spirit's gifts, which are only available in abundance through the baptism of the Spirit. He directly refers to the baptism of the Spirit in 1 Corinthians 12 more specifically, which shows that he believed in it. And in Titus 3:4-7 he speaks of being "washed" in the Holy Spirit "whom was poured out".

Water and Fire

A helpful way of learning more about the importance of being baptised in the Spirit (the fire) is studying the symbolism of / and the references to water and fire throughout the scriptures. Both are seen hand in hand in many parts of the Word - in the positive and the negative. God uses them together in regards to helping the righteous and in judging the unrighteous. Indeed, the Holy Spirit is described as being a refining fire and as living water (Luke 3:16, John 7:38-39).

God destroyed the world with water (Gen. 6-9) and then later destroyed Sodom and Gomorrah with fire (Gen. 18-19). But He also rescued Noah from the flood and Lot from the fire, because they were the only righteous ones in both situations. Jesus picks up these two events and says that the days leading up to His return would resemble the days of Noah and the days of Lot in the sense that the world would be full of sinful unbelievers who will suddenly realise too late that Jesus is real and that He is coming to judge them (Matt. 24:36-42, Luke 17:26-37).

In the final four chapters of Revelation, John refers to fire and water several times in relation to the Lord's return, the Millennial reign, the Final Judgment and the New Heaven and New Earth. In summary, there is a destructive fire awaiting the spiritual cowards, but life-giving water available for the spiritually thirsty.

In both his letters, Peter uses the same two historical examples to warn about sin and judgment in relation to the Second

Coming, but expands their usage. He uses the flood of Noah's day to help his readers understand the washing away of a person's sinfulness represented by baptism in water. He states that it represents the cleansing of our conscience brought about by Christ's death and resurrection.

Jesus had to go through the path of death, but came back out into the light of life, just as Noah and his family faced death, but God took them through and refined them by separating the wicked people from them. Peter then explains that God did not spare the world during the flood, nor the people of Sodom, yet rescued the righteous. Therefore, he will do the same for his followers today (see: 1 Pet. 3:18-22; 4:4-5 and 2 Pet. 2:5-8, Jude 0:7).

Peter also reminds believers not to be surprised by the fiery trial they are going through, but rather to be thankful as they can draw closer to Christ through it (1 Pet. 4:12-19). He later makes clear that in fitting with His promise not to destroy the world by water, God would instead destroy it by fire (see all of 2 Pet. 3).

One of the Psalmists wrote:

...O God, have tested us; you have tried us as silver is tried. You brought us into the net; you laid a crushing burden on our backs; you let men ride over our heads; we went through fire and through water; yet you have brought us out to a place of abundance.

Psalm 66:10-12
(see also: Prov. 17:3).

In similar fashion, God encourages His faithful people through Isaiah that He would save them and be with them through the water and the fire. The passage is so comforting and can be applied to any believer living today. The words were a favourite of Ray Granner (one of the two people whom this book is dedicated to) and were quoted at his cremation service in 2015:

> But now thus says the Lord, he who created you, O Jacob, he who formed you, O Israel: "Fear not, for I have redeemed you; I have called you by name, you are mine. When you pass through the waters, I will be with you; and through the rivers, they shall not overwhelm you; when you walk through fire you shall not be burned, and the flame shall not consume you. For I am the Lord your God, the Holy One of Israel, your Saviour.
>
> Isaiah 43:1-3

Of course, the prophet Daniel literally went through a fire, but was not burned. The 'fourth man in the fire' was with him (Dan. 3). Many years before, God spoke to Moses in the burning bush, yet the bush was not consumed (Exod. 3). Moses would later describe the glory of the Lord on the mountain as like a "devouring fire" and that those who persistently turn away from Him are consumed by that fire.

The righteous, however are refined by it (Exod. 24:17, Deut. 9:3, Luke 12:49-50, 2 Cor. 8:7, Heb. 12:29, 1 Pet. 1:3-9). God sent a pillar of fire to protect the Israelites from the attacking Egyptians and then took them through the baptising waters of the Red Sea (Exod. 13-14). Their crossing from slavery to Egypt through fire and water and into a new life and point towards a new believer's walk from slavery to sin, through two baptisms into their new life in Christ (Rom. 6).

I believe Paul provides the most helpful explanation of what God's fire means:

> Now if anyone builds on the foundation with gold, silver, precious stones, wood, hay, straw - each one's work will become manifest, for the Day will disclose it, because it will be revealed by fire, and the fire will test what sort of work each one has done. If the work that anyone has built on the foundation survives, he will receive a reward. If anyone's work is burned up, he will suffer loss, though he himself will be saved, but only as through fire.
>
> 1 Corinthians 3:12-15

Paul later reminds Timothy to "fan into flame the gift of God, which is in you through the laying on of my hands, for God gave us a spirit not of fear but of power and love and self-control." (2 Tim. 1:6-7). For a person to receive the gifts of the Spirit and fan them into flame, a Spirit-filled believer must lay hands on them and pray for them to be baptised in the fire of the Holy Spirit. When the Spirit was first poured out on the masses, He came as a fire which separated and rested on all the heads of the first believers (Acts 2:3).

The highly popular trilogy of books - *The Lord of the Rings*, written by J.R.R Tolkien (1892 - 1973) contains many Christian themes. Tolkien was a Professor of English who imparted much of his Catholic / Christian understanding into his works. *The Lord of the Rings* (and the well-loved prequel *The Hobbit*) features the character of Gandalf. In the story, which is set in the fictional world of Middle Earth, Gandalf appears as a wizard, but is actually one of five angelic beings sent by the Creator to counter the threat of Sauron (who represents Satan). Sauron actually appears as a lidless fiery eye.

In the first book of the trilogy - *The Fellowship of the Ring*, Gandalf leads the group in a quest to destroy Sauron's 'ring of power', which was forged in fire. At one point in their journey they have to travel in a deep part under a mountain. They encounter a creature called a Balrog, which was a huge, devilish, fiery being known as "a demon of the ancient world". Gandalf - being a spiritual being has power to confront this Balrog. This is what Tolkien writes about their dramatic confrontation:

"You cannot pass," he said.
The orcs stood still, and a dead silence fell.
"I am a servant of the Secret Fire, wielder of the flame
of Anor.
You cannot pass.
The dark fire will not avail you, flame of Udûn.
Go back to the Shadow!
You cannot pass."

(Tolkien, 1954a (2001))

Gandalf makes reference to the "Secret Fire", which gives him the "flame of Anor", in comparison to the Balrog's "dark fire" which gives a "flame of Udûn". In the great 2001 film adaptation of this book, the Balrog is pictured wielding a fiery sword, which resembles a flame. In the Middle Earth mythos, 'Anor' was another name for the 'Undying Lands', i.e. Heaven, whereas Udûn was a name for the Underworld or Hell (LOTR Wiki). In a conversation with American author Dr. Clyde Samuel Kilby (1902-1986), Prof. Tolkien explained that the 'Secret Fire' was meant to help explain how the Holy Spirit was sent by God the Father and into the secret inner part of all believers (Kilby, 1976).

When you think about it, Gandalf fought fire with fire (a holy fire against an evil fire), which in the real world is what we do. As we grow in our walk with Christ, the fire of His Holy Spirit should dwell in our inner being, refining us by consuming all that is sinful in our lives and all that would have once led us to the fires of Hell.

In the Bible, there was always a fire lit in the tabernacle (Lev. 6:13) and of course we are called "the Temple of the Holy Spirit", whose fire should be lit within us. As quoted above, Paul reminds Timothy to "fan the flame of God, which is in [him]" in order to conquer the spirit of fear, which comes from the Devil.

Back to *The Lord of the Rings* - Gandalf fought the Balrog known as a demon and a form of devilry and boldly pronounced its evil would not come any further. He struck his staff down in front of the Balrog in a Moses-like fashion making a clear statement. We battle the enemy every day and must not allow the Devil or his demons to come beyond a certain point. In the Bible, John writes of the Devil:

> Then another sign appeared in heaven: an enormous red dragon...the accuser of our brothers and sisters, who accuses them before our God day and night, has been hurled down. They triumphed over him by the blood of the Lamb and by the word of their testimony they did not love their lives so much as to shrink from death...the devil has gone down to you! He is filled with <u>fury</u>, because he knows that his time is short.'

See all of: Revelation 12

In *The Lord of the Rings* story, Gandalf dies after fighting the Balrog. The Creator gives Gandalf's life back so that he can complete his mission. He is strengthened and renewed so that he will be ready for even darker times ahead. He returns as 'Gandalf the White' stating that he fell "through fire and...water" (Tolkien, 1954b (2001)). He is spiritually reborn and reappears in radiant white, which may resemble the risen Christ appearing to John in Revelation. All these scenes are best seen in the highly popular and well-made film adaptions.

Those who are very familiar with the *Middle Earth* stories will probably know that there were many powerful rings made for the leaders of the various races. The one master ring forged by Sauron was secretly made to control the wearers of the others and the subsequent races. However, three of the rings were untouched by Sauron - the Ring of Fire worn by Gandalf (which ties in with his reference to being a wielder of fire), the Ring of Water worn by the Lady Galadriel and the Ring of Air worn by Elrond. Notice the fire and water together. In the third of the Hobbit trilogy of movies entitled *The Battle of the Five Armies* (2014), Sauron has captured Gandalf so that the other two ring bearers would come to his aid. Sauron hopes to identify who they are and capture all three rings to increase his power. Thankfully he fails to do that.

Before that, in the second Hobbit movie - *The Desolation of Smaug* (2013), just before Gandalf is captured, he is confronted by Sauron's chief warrior - Azog, who boldly proclaims that "[Sauron] is everywhere [for] We are legion!" That resembles words used in Christ's encounter with the demon-possessed man. The demons speak through the man saying, "My name is Legion...for we are many." (Mark 5:1-20). Going further backwards to the first Hobbit film, *An Unexpected Journey* (2012), Gandalf speaks of how important it is that there are good watchmen, "...for always Evil will look to find a foothold in this world".

In the scriptures, we are told:

> ...do not give the devil a foothold. Anyone who has been stealing must steal no longer... The thief comes only to steal and kill and destroy; [but Jesus] come that they may have life, and have it to the full...Be alert and of sober mind. Your enemy the devil prowls around like a roaring lion looking for someone to devour.

Submit yourselves, then, to God. Resist the devil, and he will flee from you. Come near to God and he will come near to you...Resist him, standing firm in the faith, because you know that the family of believers throughout the world is undergoing the same kind of sufferings...Stand firm then, with the belt of truth buckled round your waist, with the breastplate of righteousness in place, and with your feet fitted with the readiness that comes from the gospel of peace. In addition to all this, take up the shield of faith, with which you can <u>extinguish all the flaming arrows of the evil one</u>. Take the helmet of salvation and <u>the sword of the Spirit, which is the word of God</u>. And <u>pray in the Spirit on all occasions</u> with all kinds of prayers and requests. With this in mind, be alert and always keep on praying for <u>all</u> the Lord's people.

Ephesians 4:27, John 10:10, 1 Peter 5:8-9;

James 4:7-8, Ephesians 6:14-19

The word 'foothold' is 'topos' in the original Greek New Testament. It is where we get the word 'topography' from - the study of geographical features. The word 'topos' can mean a 'place'. Therefore, Paul is warning us not to give a place in our mind, heart or life to the Devil. We can throw open the door to his influences through bitterness, forgiveness, judgmental attitudes, selfishness and all other attitudes and actions that are "contrary to the Spirit".

The key to "walk[ing] in the Spirit" and keeping "in step" with Him, is to overcome that spirit of fear (Gal. 5:13-26). The battle of our lives is in the mind and the heart. Paul rightly shows us that if we continually pray instead of worrying and if we dwell on good and holy things we will guard our hearts and our minds in Christ Jesus (see: Phil. 4:2-20).

Peter says we must maintain a spiritually clean mind "so that [we] may pray" more effectively. He continues: "Each of you should use whatever gift you have received to serve others, as faithful stewards of God's grace in its various forms. If anyone speaks, they should do so as one who speaks the very words of God." (see: 1 Pet. 4:7-11)

Paul also makes clear above that the sword of the Spirit is the Word of God. Therefore, the Word is a weapon - but must be used through the Spirit and not in a humanistic, fleshly way. We must "rightly hand[le] the Word of truth" with "the Spirit of truth" and remember that Christ who lives in us is greater "than he that is in the world" (2 Tim. 2:15, 1 John 4:1-6).

Jesus set us a great example when tempted by the Devil - who purposefully twisted the Word of God. He didn't argue, but rather "led by the Spirit" He correctly quoted back truths from the Word and the Devil eventually fled him (Luke 4:1-13). The scriptures above state that he will flee if we resist him.

The Holy Spirit is the one who speaks the truths of God. To overcome that natural tendency to sin and to mistreat others, we must humbly and continually ask the Holy Spirit of God to change us from within. To use the Sword of the Spirit effectively, we must get to know the Word of God through daily study and so greater understand the words of God inspired by the Spirit. This will help us conquer our own personal struggles; better notice deception and help to keep the enemy at bay.

When Peter couldn't bear the idea of Jesus suffering and dying (and perhaps the thought that he might have to die also) he rebuked him! Jesus boldly retorted: "Get behind me, Satan!" because he was not speaking the words or thoughts of God, but of the world, the flesh and the Devil. There is a great cost to following Jesus and being convicted of sin by His Spirit (Matt. 16:21-26, John 14:17, 2 Cor. 4, 2 Tim. 3:12).

Have you counted the cost? You and I will have to go through many fiery trials that we wouldn't have if we had not committed ourselves to Christ. Consider this: before you travel to some destinations of the world where there is a threat of cholera, you have to get cholera injection. It may cause you to get sick because you've been injected with a little bit of it, but the body can fight that amount. That little bit of suffering will prevent you from the much greater risk of contracting cholera and dying.

The cost of not following Christ and rejecting Him is eternal separation from God and suffering in the fires of Hell. Following Christ and enduring to the end will result in enteral closeness with God and enjoyment in the glory of Heaven (John 3:16-21; 15:6-8; Rev. 20-22).

Receiving the Spirit and Salvation

I received the baptism of the Spirit when I was 7 soon after coming to Christ. As I recall, it was due to being taken to church which was pastored by Paul Miller (one of the two people this book is dedicated to). However, I did not commit more to Christ or grow until I was 14. I was not baptised in water until I was 21 and the beginnings of this book began when I was 28! Every seven years something great seems to happen! I wonder what will happen when I'm 35! By no means am I into numerology and obsessing about 'Biblically-significant numbers'. It is just that my life seems to have gone that way and there is Biblical significance to certain numbers - namely the number 7.

In the Book of Acts, the baptism of the Spirit seems to so often happen very soon after someone comes to Christ and are baptised in water (see: Acts 2; 8; 11:1-18; 19:1-7). Jesus Himself received the baptism of the Spirit when He was baptised in the waters of the Jordan (Matt. 3:16). I was fortunate to be baptised in the Spirit soon after my conversion to Christ, but as aforesaid, I wasn't baptised in water until much later. That was because I didn't have the right teaching and therefore didn't have the right understanding until much later. Most people get baptised in water soon after becoming a believer, but do not fully experience the baptism in the Spirit.

Do the Scriptures say that believers receive the Holy Spirit when they are born again or do they receive the Spirit later?

A number of Christians state that believing in Jesus and receiving His Spirit are different. They state that when you believe in Jesus, you are born again, but His Spirit does not enter you until you get *baptised* in the Spirit. A notable proponent of this belief is David Pawson. I have a lot of respect for His teaching and quote him in this book, yet I disagree with him on this point. Let me explain.

In John 3, Jesus said unless a person is "born of the Spirit" they "cannot enter the Kingdom of God". He uses the phrase "born again" and "born of the Spirit" interchangeably (see: John 3:3-8, 34). Therefore, His Spirit must come into us at the moment of believing in Jesus (when we are born again). This shows that the Spirit of God is involved in bringing us to salvation. He is involved in creating life (Gen 1:2; Job 33:4) and also spiritual life.

He is calling people everywhere and in those moments when we ponder the existence of God and open up a little to Him, the Spirit can reach us. He comes into the world to convict the world of sin and draw people towards a saving knowledge of Christ Jesus (John 16:8; 2 Cor. 2:16, Tis. 3:4-7). The Holy Spirit is the Spirit of Jesus calling people back to the Father, just as Jesus did whilst on Earth (John 12:32, Heb. 3:7-8).

The Spirit of Jesus comes into the born again believer. As with water baptism, the baptism of the Spirit is an outward sign of that new birth, but not an essential part of salvation. It is the outward completion of the inward reception. The thief on the cross died without being baptised in the Spirit or in water, and yet Jesus offered Him eternal life because he was repentant and acknowledged who Jesus was (Luke 23:39-43). =

Here is an example of someone who I had the honour of bringing to the Lord many years ago. After explaining the gospel, praying with him over the phone and getting him to repeat the necessary words after me and the 'Amen', there was a pause. Then unexpectedly a few seconds later, my friend said "ooh, I just feel so light all of a sudden". He said such a weight had been lifted. He had been forgiven. Neither of us expected him to say all that and it was interesting just hearing it over the phone. He was a different person and he felt that Jesus was now with Him in a spiritual way. I saw him the next day at church and he was full of confidence. Something entered Him that changed His countenance. He didn't just believe in Jesus, He also received the Spirit of Jesus there and then. Sadly, he never got baptised in the Spirit or water.

A lot of Christians recall the moment they were born again. They often experience a certain release and/or warmth. They sense God's presence - His Spirit in them. That new sense of lightness of spirit is surely the Spirit of God cleansing the new believer of the sin they have repented of and then entering their body. Jesus said, "if the Son sets you free, you are free indeed" (John 8:36) and Paul says, "where the Spirit of the Lord is, there is freedom." (2 Cor. 3:17).

If Jesus is no longer on Earth, and people are cleansed at new birth in Him, it must be by the Holy Spirit who is on Earth who does this. It cannot be just a case of believing in Jesus with nothing going on inside. Part of the Spirit's role is to bring new physical and spiritual life and to sanctify people who have been born again (Gen. 2:7, Job 33:4, John 3:6, 1 Thes. 2:13, 1 Pet. 1:2).

Paul says in order to commit to Jesus you must be able to say with your mouth "Jesus is Lord" (Rom. 10:9), then later he says that "no one can say "Jesus is Lord" except in the Holy Spirit." (1 Cor. 12:3). So, the Holy Spirit must come into us and have a role in our "born again" experience when we first accept Christ. We believe and receive together.

Paul also says we have to believe in our hearts "that God raised him from the dead" and when we do, I believe Jesus does come to live in us, by the Spirit. The belief in our hearts means we receive something back into our hearts. If you believe someone is going to give you a £5 note, you expect to receive it. Many Christian leaders claim that it is unscriptural to say, "Receive Jesus into your heart" or "Jesus comes to live inside you when you put your faith in Him", but consider the below scriptures.

John states in the opening of his gospel that "to all who did <u>receive</u> Him, to those who <u>believed</u> in His name, He gave the right to become children of God" (John 1:12). The 'receive' and the 'believe' are together. Yes, John is talking about Jesus's time on Earth - in the past tense, but the same surely applies now.

David Pawson points out that in the Gospels, people had to receive Jesus, but from Acts to Revelation, people are told to "receive the Spirit" (David Pawson - Charismatics and Evangelicals,

2016), yet Paul says in Colossians 2:6: "you received Christ Jesus the Lord, so walk in him..."

Speaking of all present and future followers, Jesus said:

- "...If anyone loves me, he will keep my word, and my Father will love him, and we will come to him and make our home with him" (John 14:23)
- "...Whoever abides in me and I in him, he it is that bears much fruit..." (John 15:5)
- "I have made you (the Father) known to them, and will continue to make you known in order that the love you have for me may be in them and that I myself may be in them." (John 17:26)

Paul said:

- "I no longer live, but Christ lives in me" (Gal. 2:20)
- "Do you not realise that Christ Jesus is in you...?" (2 Cor. 13:5)
- "...Christ in you, the hope of glory... I strenuously contend with all the energy Christ so powerfully works in me... So then, just as you received Christ Jesus as Lord, continue to live your lives in him" (Col. 1:17, 29; 2:6).
- "...through His Spirit in your inner being Christ may dwell in your hearts" (Eph. 3:16-17)

So, we are in Him and He is in us. In his first letter, John picks up Jesus' words above: "Whoever keeps his commandments abides in God, and God in him. And by this we know that he abides in us, by the Spirit whom he has given us." (1 John 3:24). Later, he says, "...the one who is <u>in you</u> is greater than the one who is in the world." (1 John 4:4, see also: 13-16).

Then, in Revelation, John records that the church in Laodicea was shutting Jesus out. Jesus' message to them is that He is knocking at the door of their church and desires to be welcomed in. Even though that applies to that situation and to that church, it can also apply to us as individuals and to groups (see also: Eph. 2:21-22). Christ is wanting to come in and dwell in us. Our bodies are the temple (the house/the church) of His Spirit (1 Cor. 3:16; 6:19, 1 Pet. 2:4-6). Jesus also says to the church in Laodicea that for anyone who does open the door to Him - "I will come <u>into</u> him" (see: Rev. 3:14-22).

So, as you can see, all throughout the scriptures we are encouraged to receive Jesus into our lives and our hearts. He comes into us by His Spirit, as He is not on the Earth anymore. Still there is more to be said. As Paul says in Romans:

> You...[are]...in the Spirit, if in fact the Spirit of God dwells in you. <u>Anyone who does not have the Spirit of Christ does not belong to him</u>. But if <u>Christ is in you</u>, although the body is dead because of sin, the Spirit is life because of righteousness. <u>If the Spirit of him who raised Jesus from the dead dwells in you</u>, he who raised

Christ Jesus from the dead will also give life to your
mortal bodies <u>through his Spirit who dwells in
you</u>...[A]ll who are led by the Spirit of God are sons of
God. For you did not receive the spirit of slavery to fall
back into fear, but <u>you have received the Spirit of
adoption as sons</u>, by whom we cry, "Abba! Father!"
<u>The Spirit himself bears witness with our spirit that we
are children of God</u>, and if children, then heirs - heirs
of God and <u>fellow heirs with Christ</u>,

Romans 8:9-11

Jesus had the Spirit remaining on Him, leading Him, with
Him, filling Him and empowering Him (see: Luke 4 and John 1:32-
34). This is what we all need. Unfortunately, many Churchgoers get
stuck at one stage of the journey and miss out on the fullness that
God is offering them by His Spirit.

I believe we must go back to Acts 2, where we see all that
God offers us. Here, hordes of people ask Peter what they must do
to be saved, He says: "Repent and be baptized every one of you in
the name of Jesus Christ for the forgiveness of your sins, and you
will receive the gift of the Holy Spirit." (Acts 2:38).

The reception of the Spirit was as a result of repenting,
believing and being baptised into Jesus. They would have been
baptised in the Spirit there and then like all the other believers,
which should actually be the norm, but sadly as David Pawson *does
rightly point out*, many Christians do not experience that. Due to a
lack of good teaching and explanation, many receive the Spirit on

some level at new birth, but miss not a fuller experience.

Yet, Jesus commanded His Disciples to baptise people in the name of the Father, the Son and the Spirit (Matt. 28:19-20). In other words, they were to introduce people to God fully and not let them miss out on anything.

For me, a clear way of explaining all this is as follows:

- We confess our sins to God, who is our Father and Creator.
- We confess Jesus Christ as our Lord who died to save us from our sins and rose again to offer us eternal life. The work of the cross is then applied into our lives and so God can forgive us. This forgiveness takes place as He replaces our unholiness with His Holy Spirit - His fruit and gifts develop as we grow in our faith.

Then as a public sign of our new birth in Him:

- We get baptised in water - which represents our cleansing from sin.

Through the Prophet Ezekiel, God spoke of a time He would empower people with His Spirit:

I will give you a new heart and put a new spirit in you; I will remove from you your heart of stone and give you a heart of flesh. "I will put My Spirit within you and cause you to walk in My statutes…"

Ezekiel 36:26-27

We need the Spirit in us from new birth in order for us to follow all of God's statutes. Yet, if we look again at Acts 19 (quoted at the outset of this book), we read of a time when the Apostle Paul meets a group of believers living in Ephesus who have NOT received the Spirit. He asks them, "Did you receive the Holy Spirit when you believed?" (Notice, the 'receive' and 'believe' together again). They say they did not hear about a Holy Spirit and had only received John's baptism. So how can a believer not have the Spirit in them?

The fact is they had not yet fully believed in Christ. They did not know about His saving work (or the Holy Spirit's indwelling) until they had met Paul. They were disciples who had repented and believed, yes, but only in response to John the Baptist's ministry, not that of Christ's.

Paul also asks them if they had been baptised in water. The Ephesians say they had only had water baptism with John to which responds by saying that John's baptism in water was just a preparation for the Messiah. So, Paul baptises them in water, in the name of Jesus and then prays over them to receive the baptism in the Spirit.

It is through reading the preceding chapter – Acts 18 that we discover why it was these men had not fully heard or believed the full Gospel. There, the Apostle Apollos, had been preaching in Ephesus, however, "he knew only the baptism of John" (see: verses 24-25). The only information Apollos had about Jesus was what he had heard from John - that Jesus was the Messiah, but nothing aout

Jesus' atoning death and resurrection. Indeed, John had been killed before this anyway (Luke 9:9).

So, the Ephesians did not know about Jesus' death and resurrection and so could not become born-again, Spirit-filled Christians. Yet, two people in Ephesus who did know - Priscilla and Aquila take Apollos aside and "explained to him the way of God more adequately" (Acts 18:26).

As I say, many people are spiritually stuck at one level or another due to a lack of knowledge. I remember the very first talks I ever gave, which were back in 2005. The subject of the teachings was actually the Holy Spirit and were delivered to a local prayer-group I was a part of then. The talks were only five minutes long and were in fact mere introductions to a tape teaching series that we were listening to.

Several people there had been born again believers for many years and had long shown Godly fruits of the Spirit, yet they only got more fully baptised in the Spirit as a response to the two talks.

Being filled with the Spirit is an ongoing and repeated experience, for we do become dry sometimes in our spiritual journey – this is often due to sin. In his letter to the Ephesians, Paul says not to allow sin to settle in their lives, but instead "be filled with the Spirit" (Ephesian 5:18). The Greek wording he used indicate the 'present continuous sense' and do not refer to a one-time experience. Bearing in mind, Paul was speaking to believers who had already got the Spirit. So, he was saying that they had to be *continually* filled with the Spirit.

Paul describes the Holy Spirit is described as being like a deposit, and sometimes we need more deposits put into our spiritual account (see: 2 Cor. 1:21-22, 2 Cor. 5:5, 2 Tim. 1:14). We must continually ask the Father for more of His Holy Spirit to fill us.

The Spirit works in different ways for different people. Only He knows when someone has been truly born again - when that moment occurred. Only He can search and know all things. It is a mystery that we struggle to grapple with. We just cannot fully and adequately explain the whole experience.

I remember being baptised in the Spirit at 7 or 8; then taking God, His Word and a potential ministry more seriously as a teen and finally getting baptised in water at the age of 21, yet I personally cannot remember the moment I came to Christ. It is as though I always believed. Therefore, the famous hymn lyrics, "How precious did that grace appear the hour I first believed." do not mean the same for me as for many others (Newton, 1779).

I just know a person must be born again to enter God's Kingdom and that is important to show that the world that you have been separated from it by being baptised in water and in the Spirit. The old nature is no good. It is corrupt. It needs replacing with something immeasurably and incomparably greater, holier and with something that will last forever. It is only something that God our Father offers, through the atoning death of His Son and made possible through His eternal Spirit who empowers us to live the amazing Christian life.

Jesus did not die on that cross to give us a new brand of misery or just a new religion to replace the old one. As He said Himself, He came to give us life and life to the full (John 10:10). It is by His Spirit who gives life (Rom. 8:10-15), so if you need filling or refilling with the Spirit, then humbly ask God to give more of His Spirit and to highlight areas of your life that you need to change, which are blocking Him.

Many Christians are stuck in the 10 days between Christ's ascension and Pentecost. Many preachers go on and on about Christ's triumph through the Cross, the resurrection and His ascension back to glory. Yet, they lack the empowering Spirit within them. The Cross, the resurrection and the ascension are the foundation stones of our faith and should never be moved or forgotten, yet we often keep returning there with nothing new to say. We need the Spirit to bring that truth to the fore along with all that God wants to say here - now for you and me.

The disciples did not start preaching the Gospel straight after Jesus ascended. They needed the Spirit's power to equip them. They knew the Word, but they needed to know the Spirit too. As Paul Miller once said: "There's a difference between knowing the truth [in your mind] and having that truth empowered in your heart." (Paul Miller, 2011).

Are there notable differences between Christians baptised in the Spirit and those who haven't been?

Yes. You can often tell. The non-Spirit-baptised tend to less joyful, a bit more legalistic, and don't seem to understand certain spiritual things. They usually don't feel led to raise their hands or clap in worship times. There isn't that freedom. They often struggle with subjects like the end-times and prophecy, and usually don't seem to want to know. They tend to see things too black and white (morally-speaking). By no means am I criticising them for trying to true to the Word, but they actually fail to see that to be baptised in the Spirit *is* Biblical and is for every believer.

If you are preaching to them they are more likely to be ever-so-serious in the face, whereas as baptised in the Spirit people will usually nod, be more animated and have more visible joy. Something in what you're saying will resonate with their spirit on a deep level. As Paul says, "where the Spirit of the Lord is, there is freedom" (2 Cor. 3:17) They feel that desire and freedom to clap and raise their hands in worship.

There is an internal freedom when the believer is baptised in the Spirit. There's a place and a space in our hearts for the Spirit. One of the marks of the early church and in modern day revivals is the liberty of the people. You see, God wants to set people free from the bondage of sin. He wants them to have an inner joy and peace to be free to live with Him that nothing outside can destroy (unless we let it).

That is why the Spirit convicts us of our sin, because sin holds us bondage, but the Spirit gives life and liberty (Rom. 8:15). God through the Spirit's infilling brings the immediacy of His presence into our lives. We must cooperate with Him.

I do however, look up to many non-baptised in the Spirit believers (i.e. many evangelicals) because they can sometimes be more mature, balanced and faithful to the Lord, despite being without that empowering and fuller infilling of the Spirit. Now, Spirit-filled believers (i.e. many charismatics) sometimes get too hyped up and lose sight of the scriptures. It is by no means the Holy Spirit causing them to be over the top, it is themselves or some other influence (sadly sometimes demonic).

In 2 Corinthians 11:3-15, Paul warns about receiving a different spirit than the one true Holy Spirit. He also gives instructions on maintaining order in church services so as to prevent behaving in a wacky, unspiritual and even insulting way before the Lord (see all of: 1 Cor. 11-12 and 14). Some Christians enter into 'charismaia', rather than the charismatic.

Similarly, there can be a difference between 'faithful people' and 'people of faith'. You might think: Aren't they the same? Well, not necessarily. Faithful Christians will be more attentive to church; to the reading of the Word; to prayer and to carrying out their God-given duties. They however struggle to have faith in situations to believe in the gifts and in healing and miracles etc.

Now, people of faith tend to believe more in the spiritual gifts, in the power of God to heal, do amazing miracles and to transform people and even nations, yet they sometimes fail to stay grounded in church, the Word, prayer and being consistent with their God-given duties. They may say, "I haven't felt the Holy Spirit calling me to visit the sick", when in fact the Bible called all people to do that (Matt. 25:36, Jas. 5:13-15).

Now, in Acts, Luke tells us that the 120+ believers who first received the Spirit's infilling did the following things. The devoted themselves to the apostles' teaching, regular fellowship in homes and at the temple, to the breaking of bread, to prayer, to believing in the miracles and to generous giving to the poor. You see, they were people of faith and of faithfulness. Indeed, only faith can please God (Heb. 11:3) and faithfulness is a fruit of God's Spirit - who is faithful to us (Gal. 5:22). We need both.

Other reasons why people do not always receive the
baptism of the Spirit?

I have heard and seen many Christians who do not seem to receive much of the Spirit's baptism or perhaps they have been baptised, but they have but have not experienced being filled with the Spirit. They have not fanned into flame God's gifts nor have they been stirred up in the faith again by His Spirit. They have grown a little old and cold in their faith. They need a renewal and revival. Why does this happen?

A lack of faith due to fear and doubt can lead to this. It is impossible to be in right relationship with God if you do not have faith in Him (Heb. 11:6). How then can you receive more of His Holy Spirit in you if you doubt Him or fear? With some people they perhaps have unrepented sin and so the Spirit cannot move into a spiritual neighbourhood where there is sin present.

This is different to someone battling with sinful strongholds, who know they are wrong and want deliverance. Hebrews 3 encourages us not to harden our hearts due to sin but to soften them through repentance and adhering to the voice of the Holy Spirit. If you feel this may be appropriate for you then please read Hebrews 3.

The Spirit can be withheld due to divisions and discord amongst believer's. In Acts 8, the Apostle Philip preaches the Gospel to a group of Samaritans. It was the first time they had heard the Gospel and many of them come to know Christ. The Jews and the Samaritans had hated each other for centuries and the Samaritans there do not receive the baptism of the Spirit until Peter and John (two Jews) arrive.

The delay of the Spirit's baptism was a sign to all those there that regardless of their longstanding ethnic and religious differences they all could receive the same Holy Spirit, who comes to unite all believers in the truth of the Gospel. Jesus had once said to a Samaritan woman at the well that all those who worship the true and living God must do it "in Spirit and in truth" (John 4:1-26). The Spirit is for everyone, for He was "poured out on <u>all</u> flesh" (Acts 2:17-18).

Finally, I would say that false teaching or lack of any teaching on the reception / gifts / baptism of the Spirit can prevent a person from receiving. More specifically, a Christian may have been in a church which teaches cessationist beliefs, is over ritualistic, is obsessed with the supernatural and preaches a false Gospel; where there is an over emphasis on tradition which quenches the Spirit or just a Word-heavy church with no life of the Spirit there. For more on this and on what I believe are false teachings on the gifts of the Spirit i.e. cessationism, see: the final chapter.

How do I receive?

The first people to receive the baptism of the Spirit followed Christ obediently (Acts 1-2) and they themselves told the first Christian converts to repent of all their sin (Acts 2:37) and receive the Spirit through the laying on of hands (Acts 19:6). Those who did repent had a desire to receive the baptism of the Spirit. They had faith in God.

So, I would encourage anyone to ask the Father to guide them by His Spirit into a good, balanced communion of believers and ask for direction and discernment. Then to approach the leaders about wanting to be baptised in the Spirit with an expectant hope. Sometimes the outward evidence of receiving the Spirit comes straight away or sometimes days later.

Do not tense up and worry about not being baptised (or not being worthy). God will often speak to a person or fill them up with His Spirit when they are at peace and have faith in Him. We stress out about not hearing from Him and it is often because we are stressing out. We are blocking His voice. The same can be said for receiving His Spirit in more of His fullness. An important thing to do is to relax and be patient before the Lord your God.

5.

THE GIFTS OF THE SPIRIT

"Our talents are the gift that God gives to us. What we make of our talents is our gift back to God."

Leo Buscaglia

The original Greek word for 'gift' (as in a 'spiritual gift') in the New Testament is 'charism', where we get the word 'charisma' and 'charismatic' from. Charismatic Christians are the main proponents of the gifts of the Spirit, although other Christian groups teach the need to use them too. Despite the lack of teaching in many quarters of Christendom on the gifts of the Spirit, the Bible tells us a lot about them.

In Exodus 31, we read of a man called Bezalel who was said to have the Spirit of God in him. The Spirit inspired him with all kinds of craftsmanship and artistic designs, which He used for God. This shows how the Spirit gives inspiration and channels and anoints our natural God-given abilities to glorify God and serve others.

Way back in the days when the Psalms were being written, it was prophesied that the Lord would one day ascend on high and then give gifts to His people (see: Paul's teaching on this in Eph. 4.8-13). This is what happened. After Jesus ascended back to Heaven, He asked the Father to send the Holy Spirit in order to supernaturally equip all believers with spiritual gifts (John 14:16; 16:7, Acts 1:1-11).

Jesus Himself said: "If you then, being evil, know how to give good gifts to your children, how much more will your heavenly Father give the Holy Spirit to those who ask Him!" (Luke 11:13). Matthew's version of these words of Christ have Him saying that the Father would give "good gifts to those who ask Him" (Matt. 7:11). Put tougher we can see that it is the Father gives the gifts and does it by actually giving His Holy Spirit to those who ask for Him to live inside them! How amazing is that!

James said that "every good and perfect gift comes from the Father of lights" and that the reason we don't always have these good things from God is that we don't ask, or we ask with the wrong attitude. Perhaps from a place of pride in one's on talents or jealousy of other people's gifts. James encourages humility before God and good relations with our Christian brothers and sisters (Jas. 1:17; 4:1-10).

As the very well-known evangelist, Billy Graham (1919-2018) points out in his book on the Holy Spirit - Christmas time is when parents will give gifts to their children according to their children's desires and interests. Similarly, our Heavenly Father gives us spiritual gifts through His Spirit according to our spiritual desires and interests (see: 1 Cor. 12:4, 8 and 11). The major difference is that the latter are for serving others, rather than ourselves. Children will often squabble with each other over the gifts they've been given (or not been given), just as some Christians become jealous of another person's spiritual gifts and wish they had them. But we are discouraged from behaving that way (see: 1 Cor. 12:12-31, and also: Billy Graham, (1978) 1988).

There are several places in the epistles which speak of the various gifts of the Spirit. Most of them are listed in 1 Corinthians 12-14. At the outset of that triad of chapters on the gifts, Paul makes clear: "Now about the gifts of the Spirit, brothers and sisters, I do not want you to be uninformed." (1 Cor. 12:1). Paul also explains that there is one Spirit who gives various gifts to various people as He chooses (see: 1 Cor. 12:4-13). That also shows that God holds us responsible for our use of the gifts, for example: teaching the Word is one of the gifts of the Spirit and those who use it will be judged more strictly by God than other people who do not have that gift (see: Jas. 3:1).

We must remember to be good stewards of what are actually His gifts. We are merely the caretakers. Why not ask God to reveal to you the gifts He wants you to have or use more? Perhaps study

Now, as you read earlier, there is the "fruit of the Spirit", but there are also the "gifts (plural) of the Spirit". We cannot cherry pick the spiritual fruits (excuse the pun), hence why the Bible says, "fruit" more so than "fruits". Yes, Jesus referred to them in the plural, but we must show them all as if it were one big juicy, nitrous fruit which can come in nine varieties.

Now, with the gifts, we do not receive them all - they are distributed according to our personalities, talents and abilities that God has already given us. We often say someone is gifted in music, writing or art, well, the Holy Spirit gave those gifts (Exod. 35:30-35) and can empower and anoint it so it is far more effective and is used more for the spreading of the Kingdom and to the glory of God.

Through searching the scriptures, I have found that the gifts of the Spirit are as follows:

GENERAL GIFTS	SPECIFIC GIFTS
apostleship	prophesying (this appears among the specific gifts and in more general 'gift lists' too)
evangelising	
pastoring	words of wisdom
prophesying	words of knowledge
teaching	interpreting tongues
discipling	speaking in new tongues
administrating	distinguishing between spirits
serving	driving out evil spirits
encouraging	healing
giving generously	many other miraculous powers
showing mercy	Jesus (directly and indirectly) referred to all of the last six gifts as signs that would follow those who believed in Him and worked in the power of His name (Mark 16:17-18). Though He doesn't specifically refer to 'interpreting tongues' or 'distinguishing between spirits', they are inextricably linked with the gift of speaking in new tongues and the power to drive out evil spirits.
showing and sharing faith	
helping	
guiding	

See also: Romans 12:3-8, all of 1 Corinthians 12-14, Ephesians 4:7-13, 1 Peter 4:7-11 and Heb. 2:1-4. I would encourage anyone to study those passages and see which gifts may apply to them. In addition, Isaiah prophesied that the Messiah would show godly fruit and have several gifts given by the Spirit (see: Isa. 11:1-2). Even though Jesus was God incarnate, as already mentioned in chapter 2, Jesus did not perform miracles or use any of the above gifts in His own strength - it was all by the Spirit (Matt. 12:28). Paul says that he himself did the same (Rom. 15:19, 1 Cor. 2:4).

Just as Jesus showed the whole range of the fruit of the Spirit, He also had all the gifts of the Spirit as well. He is and will always be the only one in history to have them all. Some might point out that He didn't appear to speak in tongues, nor did He interpret them, yet being God incarnate, perfect, baptised in the Spirit, and clearly possessing all the other gifts He would surely have been able to speak in different human and Heavenly languages and still does today. After all, He can hear prayers in all languages and tongues from people all over the world (Isaiah 28:11-13, Mark 5:41; 15:34, Acts 26:14).

Jesus may well have prayed in tongues privately. Mark records two occasions when Jesus sighed deeply in His spirit (Mark 7:34; 8:12). The wording in both cases appear to be similar to Paul's words about the spiritual sighing and groaning in a person's spirit which comes out of their mouth in the form of different tongues (Rom. 8:22-27).

Sadly, too many churches do not teach, encourage or even believe in the gifts of the Spirit. Some teach that (at least some of) the gifts died out with the early apostles. That belief is called cessationism. I will discuss this in much more detail in Chapter 6. Too many cessationist church leaders have been put off by the *sensationalism* of many charismatic Christians. I know the gifts haven't died out and I refuse to be put off by over-the-top Christians. God has given me gifts through His Spirit and I have seen His gifts at work in many other Christians.

Thankfully, many churches do use and display at least some of the left list of giftings, even without the baptism of the Spirit, because we can all have those God-given gifts (and non-believers have some of them because they're made in God's image), however the Holy Spirit in us enables us to do so much more with them. He brings purpose and holiness to them and helps us use them for God's glory and for the spreading of His Kingdom.

The left column above seems to list the more important gifts, as they are highlighted more throughout the New Testament and Paul refers to many of them as being "the greater gifts". He also says not everyone has all the gifts, but that we should all seek those "greater gifts" or "higher gifts" as some translations say (see: 1 Cor. 12:27-31).

Though the gifts in the right column are not as emphasised in scripture, they are key too. I have never known a non-baptised in the Spirit (non-Spirit filled) Christian to have any of the right list of gifts. Therefore, I believe the baptism in the Spirit is necessary to receive any of those more specific gifts. They are sadly harder to find in churches, as the baptism in the Spirit is usually not nearly as taught about as the baptism in water.

Let's look at three associated gifts in that right column, which are given through the Spirit's baptism: the gift of tongues, the gift of interpreting tongues and the gift of prophecy. These three specific gifts are the only three that the Bible discusses them at length. Paul addresses them particularly in 1 Corinthians 14. Most Christians seem to talk about those three gifts more than the others and they seem to divide opinion in the wider church more than any others.

The Gift of Tongues

As mentioned in the above table, the end of Mark's Gospel records how Jesus prophesied that the ability to speak in new tongues would be one of the many signs which would accompany His followers. All 120 Christian believers gathered on Pentecost morning spontaneously spoke in tongues when the Spirit came down on them. People from several different language groups around about seemed to understand what they were saying. This was fulfilling Jesus' prophecy. However, a much older prediction from the prophet Isaiah records God's own words about a future time for Israel and Jerusalem:

> For by people of strange lips and with a foreign tongue the Lord will speak to this people, to whom he has said, "This is rest; give rest to the weary; and this is repose"; yet they would not hear. And the word of the Lord will be to them...

Isaiah 28:11-13

In 1 Corinthians 14, Paul quotes part of that passage in his discussion on the gift of tongues (see: verse 21).

The original Greek word used for 'tongue(s)' in the New Testament is 'glossolalia', where we get the word 'glossary' from. Today, 'glossolalia' usually refers to the ability to speak in tongues which no one (not even the speaker) can discern, but which has a Heavenly meaning. Whereas, the term 'xenoglossia' refers to a person's ability to suddenly speak in a foreign tongue previously unknown to that person. That is what happened at Pentecost in Acts 2. At the opening of 1 Corinthians 13, Paul refers to speaking in the tongues of men and the tongues of angels (Heavenly language). I quote it further down.

So, it appears the gift of tongues can be either a discernible language to some people, or a completely undiscernible language to anyone. Either way, it is completely undiscernible by the speaker (unless an interpretation is given), but completely discernible by God in Heaven, who knows all languages (1 Cor. 14:1-2). In fact, God caused the evil people at Babel to speak languages in order to divide them, but He caused the holy people at Pentecost to widen their unity through language (again, I delve into this more deeply later in the book).

It is good to speak in tongues and be able to interpret them because:

we're told to pray in the Spirit at all times - tongues can be one of the ways	Eph. 6:18, Jude 0:20
it can be a heavenly, Godly, Spiritual language	1 Cor. 13.1, 1 Cor. 14:2
it can enable one to speak a foreign language leading others to Christ*	Acts 2:5-11; 1 Cor. 14:22
it can be a direct, edifying word from the Lord when wisely interpreted	1 Cor. 14.1
it builds people up, but it should be used by only two or three in public	1 Cor. 14:5, 14-16, 26-27
along with the other gifts it should be used, but orderly and to glorify God	1 Cor. 14:23-33, 1 Pet. 4:7-11
it should not be blocked or untaught by any church	1 Cor. 12:1, 14:1, 39
though it may sound unusual, it is from God and so therefore good	Acts 2:12-21
when you really don't know what to pray - pray in tongues, if you can	Rom. 8:26

The Holy Spirit can speak in all languages and so when we speak in tongues we can speak the very words that the Holy Spirit is saying to people at that time.

I have been in many charismatic church services and conferences where someone spontaneously speaks a word in tongues and then there's a pause as people reverently wait for the interpretation. It is an utterly amazing experience and you can just sense God's Spirit in that situation and hear God's own words being spoken for there and then! It really does edify and uplift the church.

We also must remember that as one studies Paul's teaching on it, he puts a real emphasis on the private speaking of tongues and a limitation on the use of it in church (Rom. 8:26-28, 1 Cor. 14:18-19, 27). I am aware that all 120+ believers gathered at Pentecost spoke in tongues at the same time, but that was a onetime event whereby the Spirit was poured out for the first ever time. God does not do things in half measures and He when He comes - He comes with a blast!

In our private prayer times, God can guide us on how to pray more effectively both in our own language and in other tongues. One can practise the gift in private and not hurt anyone through a false word, interpretation or tongue that wasn't even from God.

As one reads his letters, it is clear that this is because God is a God of order and so the use of tongues should be done in an orderly, edifying and truthful manner in the presence of believers and non-believers alike. Paul also says that though he desires all people to speak in tongues (1 Cor. 14:5), he recognises that not everyone does (1 Cor. 12:30), and for those that don't, God can give other gifts. No one should be pressurised to speak in tongues or to use any spiritual gift, for "...there are varieties of gifts, but the same Spirit; and there are varieties of service, but the same Lord; and there are varieties of activities, but it is the same God who empowers them all in everyone..." (See: 1 Cor. 12:4-6, 11). It is for the individual to "earnestly desire the spiritual gifts" (1 Cor. 14:1, 12).

As aforesaid, some gifts are greater and more foundational in their application than others, but no one is greater in the sight of God because of the gifts they have (1 Cor. 14:5). Paul says not to be jealous of another believer because you want to be like them and have their gifts. He used the example of body parts all being necessary to make the whole body function well and how stupid and unproductive it would be if they all started envying one other (see: 1 Cor. 12:12-31).

The Tongue

Notice that the list of gifts a few pages up all involve speaking. If God's Spirit does not grant you the gift of tongues, He will grant you other gifts all of which will probably cause you to use your mouth. This is because almost all of the spiritual gifts require us to use our mouth in order to serve God and others in a spirit of love and humility, and not to serve ourselves. They are God's gifts through His Spirit, given to all to use wisely as "good and faithful servant(s)" of Jesus (see: Matt. 25:14-30). As I said before, they don't belong to the one who is gifted, but to God.

As partially quoted above, Peter states in his first letter:

Above all, love each other deeply, because love covers over a multitude of sins. Offer hospitality to one another without grumbling. Each of you should use whatever gift you have received to serve others, as faithful stewards of God's grace in its various forms. If anyone speaks, they should do so as one who speaks the very words of God. If anyone serves, they should do so with the strength God provides, so that in all things God may be praised through Jesus Christ. To him be the glory and the power for ever and ever. Amen."

1 Peter 4:8-11

Jesus said:

> ...For the mouth speaks what the heart is full of. A good man brings good things out of the good stored up in his heart, and an evil man brings evil things out of the evil stored up in his heart.

Matthew 12:34-35

When you're full of anger - you shout.
When you're full of joy - you laugh.
When you're full of shock - you gasp
When you're full of fear - you scream.

People know more of what is in your heart the more you express yourself through words. Through the Spirit of Christ living in us and then the baptism in the Spirit, we become filled up at a heart level and then express that through the mouth. This can happen spontaneously or as a result of being prayed over. At that Pentecost, the Holy Spirit fell on the believers, "...they were all filled with the Holy Spirit and began to speak in other tongues as the Spirit gave them utterance." (Acts 2:4).

The same can be said for you or me today. When the Spirit falls on us (usually through prayer and the laying on of hands) we should begin to use gifts either already there or new ones entirely. The gifts may not be evident straight away and we may not spontaneously speak there and then, but the gifts should show as time goes on - and show verbally. We should be changed for the better and renewed. Someone could be prayed over and they may just breathe, because they've been released of something wrong in them and now the Holy Spirit can come in more fully.

The tongue (meaning the words which come out of it) is the most difficult part of your body to control, which is surely why God has given such an array of amazing spiritual gifts - all of which (in varying degrees) involve speaking good, holy, edifying things of God. Whether it be words of wisdom, knowledge, prophecy or encouragement; teaching, evangelising, speaking in tongues or whatever, you use the tongue.

Notice what the writer James says,

Know this, my beloved brothers: let every person be quick to hear, slow to speak, slow to anger...If anyone thinks he is religious and does not bridle his tongue but deceives his heart, this person's religion is worthless...the tongue is a small member, yet it boasts of great things. How great a forest is set ablaze by such a small fire! And the tongue is a fire, a world of unrighteousness. The tongue is set among our members, staining the whole body, setting on fire the entire course of life, and set on fire by hell...With it we bless our Lord and Father, and with it we curse people who are made in the likeness of God. From the same mouth come blessing and cursing...

James 1:19, 26; 3:5-6, 9-10.
see also: Proverbs 18:21; 26:18-28

So, the tongue is like a fire, therefore, we need the fire of the Holy Spirit to refine our words that come off our tongues. Isaiah spurted out eight goes on the sinful people around him, but when he is shown Heaven and his own sins are revealed he says "'Woe is me!' I cried. 'I am ruined! For I am a man of unclean lips, and I live among a people of unclean lips, and my eyes have seen the King, the Lord Almighty.'". An Angel touches his lips with charcoal as a symbolic way of cleansing him and refining his words (see: Isa. 6 and also: Prov. 25:21-22; 26:19-20).

As we listen and draw closer to the Lord, we learn more and more how and when to speak. Paul says that as part of our new life in Christ, we ought to get rid of the hardness of heart and to "speak in love" to one another. John say as to "walk in love". If we think and speak corrupting things or act in corrupt ways, we "grieve the Holy Spirit of God, by whom [we] were sealed". We must confess and repent to be re-cleansed, for God is always willing to forgive us. He understands our weaknesses (see: Eph. 4:17-32, see also: 1 Cor. 12:3, 1 John 1:9; 2 John 1:6). We are not a surprise to Him for He made us and as someone once "although God stamped His image in us sin distorts that image".

God the Father created the universe through a word, Jesus was that Word and the Holy Spirit of God gives us words. What we must be careful of is thinking we can control situations and even our own destiny by speaking certain statements "of faith" all the time. In recent decades, there has been an increasing number of 'Word of Faith' televangelists who keep promising their congregations and TV audiences blessing if they would speak prosperity and wealth and miraculous health over their lives. They get the people hyped up on false promises. Many of these preachers teach that if their congregations and viewers would hand over large amounts of cash, it will happen. Surely, they just want your money to supply their usually lavish lifestyles.

The reality is that we cannot force the hand of God and try to control what, when and how He gives us things just by commanding them into being. We have to be faithful, patient, humble and right before Him in the heart and mind. Some triumphalist Christians (as I call them) state that we are "gods" according to the scripture and so can creatively speak things into being, just as God did. Yet, when the Bible says we are "gods", it is written in a sarcastic tone (see: Psa. 82 and John 10:31-36).

Now, we are creative and there is power in the tongue, but we have to be careful that we are not entering into dodgy territory where we try to control our life through words. Are we trying to just speak certain things into existence so we have the life we want? Are our hearts ready for that which we try to command into being? Should we not just submit to God and let Him be the captain of our vessel? Let us speak His words only and apply them in the way they were intended.

This book is dedicated to Paul Miller and he was someone who gave many prophetic words of knowledge and wisdom to many churches and church groups throughout the years. His last words were given the night before he died (13th October 2015) and were to a group of young Christians near Dudley. They were a tongue interpretation. He simply felt God speaking through Him saying: "I am God and you are not" (Paul Miller, 2015).

As for me and my own experience, I received the gift of tongues (and was baptised in the Spirit) when I was only seven or eight years old. I had only just come to Christ, but didn't actually get baptised in water until I was 21. The only recorded example in the Bible of people being baptised in the Spirit before water is the group of Gentiles, including Cornelius (see: Acts 10). There, Luke also mentions that they spoke in tongues (see vs. 46) before their water baptism.

God developed the gift of tongues in me over many years and I can now speak in far more words of tongues than when I was a child. Some of the earlier words were probably not from God. I think when I was a child I just made some of them up, but eventually those nonsense words dropped off, leaving only the genuinely spiritual ones. New one ones developed as I drew closer to the Lord.

I love to pray in tongues as I really sense God's presence with me. I only pray in tongues as I feel a prompt in my spirit to. I feel a sensation in my mouth and a desire to speak them out, even though I do not always know what the words mean. I just know that they are necessary and that God understands them (see: 1 Cor. 14:14).

He has a patient, refining effect on the persevering heart. I find that there are times when I just do not know what or how to pray about something or for someone. Praying in tongues - which I don't always understand - but God does is very helpful. Somehow, I sense that the Spirit is directing me to speak the right, Godly things and I have often experienced a sense of peace about the situation afterwards.

There have been many times where I have ministered to people by praying over them in tongues and they have experienced a healing or a sense of Godly affirmation, joy or peace. The words I must be speaking in the spiritual realm must be doing something to them that is bringing about spiritual goodness in them. In those public situations, I believe it is more important for an interpretation, as per Paul's words in 1 Corinthians 14:13. I have often had an interpretation and have shared with the prayee.

The Gift of Interpreting Tongues

Alongside the gift of speaking in different tongues, comes the ability to interpret those tongues (1 Cor. 12:10; 14:5, 13). It is a good, revelatory gift which is there to edify the church body (1 Cor. 14:12). Just as language interpreters will share in a discernible language to an individual or group what a non-native speaker is saying, so too many Spirit-filled believers can interpret tongue-words spoken by the Holy Spirit through someone else.

How is this accomplished? By the Spirit! When a tongue is spoken, and an interpretation given, the words are directly from the Lord. How amazing it is to hear such a word from the Lord God Almighty! It must be like the direct words Abraham, Moses, Miriam, David, Isaiah, Daniel, Anna and the other prophetic men and women received from the Lord, which they then shared with the believers of their day.

As with the gift of tongues, the interpretation of them is addressed predominantly in Paul's first letter to the church in Corinth. The gift is a prophetic one, as seen in that letter, namely in chapter 14. It is prophetic in the sense that it can be a way of sharing words which God wants people to hear in order to remind them of His ways, to soften their hearts and to prepare them for a future time, just as God did in Biblical days. A tongue should be weighed up (especially in public settings), just as a prophecy must be as well. Indeed, as I say, prophecy can come by the way of a tongue interpretation (see: 1 Cor. 14:5-6 and also 2 Pet. 1:20-21).

In the 1 Corinthians 14 chapter, Paul emphasises the need for interpretation by using the example of musical instruments needing to play discernible melodies in order for them to be of use. He also explains that if an unbeliever were to walk into a church full of people praying in tongues with no one interpreting, it will only put them off - "will they not say that you are out of your minds?" (verses 22-25). Therefore, only two or three should speak in tongues, someone must interpret and if there is no one to interpret the congregation should pray to God about it.

The tongue-speaker can also interpret. I have seen this occur myself and although some people object to this, it is Biblical, for we read that "the one who speaks in a tongue should pray for the power to interpret." (verse 13). Paul states that someone must interpret, but if no interpretation occurs, the tongue-speaker should wait silently and patiently in reverence to God, trusting Him in the situation (verses 27-28).

A true tongue interpretation can bring guidance, conviction and comfort, as it is a perfect God speaking to a non-perfect church. Knowing our Lord Jesus, He will gently warn and woo His people back by speaking through his prophets, teachers and those who can discern tongues and spirits, as He always did in times past.

The Gift of Prophecy

Around one quarter of the Bible is made up of prophetic statements about future events. Many of the prophecies have been fulfilled, but many have not. They were spoken by a range of prophets and prophetesses across the millennia - all of whom looked towards the Messiah - Jesus Christ. The Biblical prophecies are either linked to Christ's First Coming and / or to His Second Coming in the future.

The Bible itself says that all prophecy is given by the Holy Spirit working within a believer:

> Concerning this salvation, the prophets, who spoke of the grace that was to come to you, searched intently and with the greatest care, trying to find out the time and circumstances to which the Spirit of Christ in them was pointing when he predicted the sufferings of the Messiah and the glories that would follow. It was revealed to them that <u>they were not serving themselves but you</u>, when they spoke of the things that have now been told you by those who have preached the gospel to you by the Holy Spirit sent from heaven. Even angels long to look into these things... [Now,] no <u>prophecy of Scripture</u> comes from someone's own interpretation. For no prophecy was ever produced by the will of man, but men spoke from God as they were carried along by the Holy Spirit.
>
> 1 Peter 1:10-12; 2 Peter 1:20-21

Therefore, it follows that understanding prophecy should surely be an essential element of the Christian life for all believers as we look towards His imminent return.

One of the most significant prophecies of the Bible was given through the prophet Joel by the Holy Spirit centuries before it began to be fulfilled. Joel foresaw a day when the Spirit of God Almighty would be poured out on *all* believers and not just on a few individuals, as was the way in pre-Pentecostal times. The first half of that prophecy became a reality on Pentecost Sunday c. AD 30, when the Spirit was poured out on the 120+ Christian believers. Peter - the leader of those early Christians quotes the passage of Joel's prophecy. Here is the relevant part of it:

> ...I will pour out my Spirit on all people. Your sons and daughters <u>will prophesy</u>, your old men will dream dreams, your young men will see visions... Even on my servants, both men and women, I will pour out my Spirit in those days <u>and they will prophesy</u>...

> Joel 2:28-29, Acts 2:17-18

What is striking in one sense, (although not necessarily immediately obvious) is the emphasis on the gift of 'prophecy' within that prophecy. It shows that the most clear, discernible sign of the Spirit coming will be seen in the ability of <u>all</u> men and women to speak and act prophetically in some way. In other words, a prophet is sharing a prophecy that all people will prophesy!

When the Spirit did come as recorded in Acts 2, the believers began to speak in tongues "as the Spirit gave them utterance". Tongues have a prophetic nature to them - they have current and future relevance for the people interpret them and to whom they are for. Tongues are one of the many ways a person can speak prophetically and impart something of spiritual value into another person or a group of people.

Prophecy is part of the fivefold ministry (Eph. 4:11) and although not all people are 'Prophets' with a capital 'P', I believe that all people can think, pray, speak and act in prophetic ways. Just as all people can help to shepherd (pastor), evangelise, teach and be an apostle to another person or people in some way or manner, so too all people have the potential for the prophetic. Peter's Pentecostal sermon following the Spirit's outpouring was itself prophetic - in the sense that it had a revelatory, relevant, Spirit-led nature to it. He spoke like one the Old Testament prophets with power and authority - explaining how prophecy was being fulfilled that very day.

Not only is prophecy one of the five-fold ministry of gifts - which form the foundation for all churches and other spiritual gifts, but it is also one of the "greater gifts" which we should "eagerly desire". This is because prophecy and the other greater gifts are central to every believer's spiritual walk:

> Now you are the body of Christ, and each one of you is
> a part of it. And God has placed in the church first of
> all apostles, second prophets, third teachers, then

miracles, then gifts of healing, of helping, of guidance, and of different kinds of tongues. Are all apostles? Are all prophets? Are all teachers? Do all work miracles? Do all have gifts of healing? Do all speak in tongues? Do all interpret? Now eagerly desire the greater gifts.

1 Corinthians 12:28-31

When studying the gifts of the Spirit, it is often good to start with prophecy, because it is the gift which is all about listening to God - who desires to speak to us. Jesus said to all seven churches of Revelation "Whoever has [spiritual] ears, let them hear what the Spirit says to the churches." (see: Rev. 2-3, and also: Mark 4:9). Jesus wants to speak to us, and He does it through the Spirit.

Paul says to "desire gifts of the Spirit, especially prophecy" (1 Cor. 14:1) and to Timothy, he encourages him not to neglect his gift that he received through the prophetic message when the church elders prayed over him (1 Tim. 4:14). This shows that prayerful, prophetic words spoken over you can help to affirm other gifts you have and even ones you do not have. You will sense a confirmation of this in your spirit.

You will notice how prayer and prophecies go hand in hand throughout the scriptures. Yet, prayer is not listed as a spiritual gift - it is an inbuilt ability already there for us to commune with our Father in Heaven. Prophesying *is* a gift and one of the greater gifts and the second of the five-fold ministry set of gifts. It also is a more specified gift and so therefore it ties all the other gifts together in some way.

The word 'prophecy' comes from the Greek 'prophēteía', which means to 'clarify' 'publicly expound', 'announce' and to 'assert God's mind'. That helps us to understand how it should be used to edify the church (1 Cor. 14:3-4), to expound upon the Word of God, but also to convict unbelievers of sin (1 Cor. 14:23-25). It is a revelatory gift, hence why the Book of Revelation is a book of prophecy. Yet, that was written almost 2,000 years ago, so what about prophecies today? I believe that God still bestows the gift of prophecy to and through his believers in order to reveal what He wants to say here and now.

Here is an example - in 1947, the prophet Smith Wigglesworth (1859 –1947) received a prophetic word from the Lord concerning the future of Great Britain. The crux of the message was that, "When the Word and the Spirit come together, there will be the biggest move of the Holy Spirit that the nation, and indeed, the world has ever seen." (Wigglesworth, 1947).

In line with this, it was the great evangelist, David Watson (1933-1984) who prophetically coined this saying during one of his sermons:

All Word and no Spirit we dry up,
All Spirit and no Word we blow up,
With the Spirit AND the Word we GROW UP!

Notice, that Wigglesworth was predominately known as a prophet, whereas Watson was an evangelist. Yet both spoke prophetically and both evangelised. It was that the latter who preached in a way that was prophetic for the time and place, more so than someone who gave direct prophetic words from the Lord.

Therein shows that there are two distinct types of prophesying:

- one whereby the Spirit of the Lord gives a word, a picture, a vision or a dream about the future through a prophet, (like Joel's prophecy)

- and the other type whereby someone shares a word, a picture, a vision or a dream through a sermon, a word of wisdom / knowledge or through a prayer time and which have relevant meaning to the here and now. For example, there may be a person in a church who needs physical healing of some kind. The Lord nudges someone else in the church to share that God will heal or has healed the ill person. It is just as when Jesus said such things to people because of their faith (Matt. 8:13, John 4:50).

Both types of prophecy can be conditional or unconditional. In other words:

- they can depend on a person's or people's heart response - like the people of Nineveh, whose response to Jonah's prophetic preaching would either judge or save them.

- or they are unconditional - like Christ's return, which will happen one day regardless of what we do or not do. No one can predict the date, but we can discern the times we are living in through rightly interpreting the prophetic signs God has given us in His Word and is still giving us through His prophets today.

All prophecies, regardless of how they come or who they are for should be heard, interpreted and applied correctly. Paul recommends that when a prophecy is given in a church, two or three wise people should weigh it up in the hearts and minds to see if it is from God (1 Cor. 14:29).

The Word of God should always be the measuring bar for all prophecies, as it reveals the nature of the Father, it exalts Jesus Christ and was inspired by His Holy Spirit. It must be asked whether the prophecy is edifying to the recipient(s), exalting of Christ and in the long run produces good fruit by leading people closer to God.

It is imperative not to add or take away from the prophecy, as this distorts it. God has given many a warning to leave His words as they are (Deut. 4:2; 12:32, Prov. 30:6, Rev. 22:18-19). God always communicates prophetic words of wisdom or knowledge or tongues perfectly - with clarity, authority and love, so there is no need to change what He says.

I remember a prophetic lady sharing a Word for me during a prayer time at my church. She had a picture of God's hand carrying me across waters in a boat to a different place. She shared that God was taking care of me and leading me to new places in Him. Little did she know that my brother had just booked me to go on a ferry to Ireland days earlier.

In the same prayer time, another lady had a picture of me standing in front of a ruined abbey in Ireland. She did not know that my mother had a similar prophetic picture of me about 15 years before. God gives us confirmation of His will for our lives through two or three people!

Another, more sobering reason for weighing up a prophecy is because of false prophets infiltrating the church - of which there are many warnings about in the scriptures (Isa. 44:25, Matt. 7:15-23; 24:11, 24, Acts 13:4-12, 1 John 4:1, Rev. 16:13). It was a standard practice to use two or three witnesses to discern the truth in many matters (Deut. 19:15, Matt. 18:15-20, 2 Cor. 13:1).

How do we discern a false prophet?

False prophets are people who:

- "come to you in sheep's clothing, but inwardly they are ferocious wolves." - thereby, appearing gentle and innocent, but deep down is full of deception and evil intent (Matt. 7:15, Acts 20:28-30)

- prophesy things which do not happen (Deut. 18:21-22, Acts 16:16-19)

- share false visions and hopes, and who are into divination (Jer. 23:16, Ezek. 13:9)

- share "fabricated stories" to cause people to follow them (2 Pet. 2:3)

- perform great signs and wonders (perhaps healing) to lead people astray (Matt. 24:24)

- alter the fundamental truths about Christ's humanity, divinity and sovereignty (2 Pet. 2:1, John 4:1-6)

- teach false doctrines through cunning and subtle ways (2 Pet. 2:1)

- behave in a depraved way (2 Pet. 2:2)

- are greedy for your money (1 Tim. 6:3-10, 2 Pet. 2:3)

- gather other false teachers and prophets around them "to say what their itching ears want to hear" and not what God wants to say through them (2 Tim. 4:3-4).

That list reminds me of a few televangelists who have so-called prophetic, healing ministries that purposefully make sure that they are the centre of attention and not God. They manipulate their followers into giving large swathes of cash to their ministries with the promise of financial prosperity. A concept not found in scripture. The Bible says that such people are awaiting a severe judgment for misapplying the Word and abusing people for their own advantage (2 Pet. 2:3, see also: Jas. 3:1). Such evangelists, prophets and pastors tend to live lavish lives paid for by their flock. This all teaches us that we can either be prophetic or pathetic. I know which one the Lord would want us to be.

Paul encouraged everyone to seek the ability to speak in tongues, but above all he rathered that people prophesied in some way or in some manner and to prophecy in an orderly, God-honouring way (1 Cor. 14:1, 5, 31). Though most people are not 'Prophets' per say, all people can be prophetic.

I encourage you to eagerly desire to become more like that. I am writing to myself as well. For God wants to take all of us from being a pathetic sinner chained to the world to being a prophetic saint abiding in the Word! A closer, more intimate relationship with God is what is needed. The more time we spend with Him - praying without ceasing, the more we will hear from Him and the more we will know how to think, pray, speak and act in a prophetic way!

We are living in disturbing times with more and more deception creeping into the church. The prophetic gift helps us to prepare for what is around the corner and to not fall into that deception or temptation. Tough times are ahead, but through an ever-closer relationship with Christ and a growing love for His Word, we will be led by His Spirit more and will be safe, because we will have endured to the end in the face of growing pressures to compromise (Matt. 24:13, Rev. 12:10-12).

In Paul's letter concerning deception creeping into the Corinthian church, Paul ends it with a Trinitarian statement to help the church to redress their teachings and beliefs (2 Cor. 13:14). He is prophetically providing the solution. He also encourages the Ephesian church in this way too, but at the outset of that letter (Eph. 1:17). I believe that if we hold strong to the right view of God as Father, Son and Spirit we will be kept from error.

John closes his first letter (which heavily warns against deception) by explaining to us that the Father, the Word and the Spirit testify for us (1 John 5:6-11, 18-21, see also: Matt. 28:19). It is a way of showing that to discover the will of our Heavenly Father, we must look at His Word to see what He says and what are His ways and be led by His Spirit, who confirms - or testifies the truth to us. The Spirit will remind us of the truth of His Word and the Word encourages us to be led the Spirit, drawing us ever closer to our Father in Heaven.

In Revelation, John prophetically describes an *unholy* trinity, which will appear in the final years of this world to deceive as many people as possible. It will be made up of Satan - who is the father of lies (John 8:44), the Antichrist - who will claim to the Messiah (2 Thes. 2:4) and the false prophet - who derives his power from the spirit of Satan (Rev. 16:13-14). Many believers will be persecuted under this demonic regime. Those who overcome will do it by power of the blood and by the Word of their testimony! (Rev. 12:10-12).

This carries the concept found in 1 John 5:4-8 of overcoming through faith in God and knowing that the Spirit, the water, the blood, the Word and the Father all testify for us that we are in the truth. They are our testimony! If we hold fast to those Gospel truths without turning to the right or to the left, we will be saved (Deut. 5:32, Matt. 24:13, 1 Cor. 15:2-4, 2 Peter 2:20-22).

We also read in Revelation how those very Christians overcame because "they did not love their lives so much as to shrink from death" (see: 12:11, see also: 1 John 2:26-29). In other words, they selflessly resisted falling foul of the unholy trinity of Satan, the Antichrist and the false prophet, but also did not give in to the fleshly trinity of 'me, myself and I'.

They knew the Father in whom there is no shifting shadows (James 1:17), they put their faith in Christ who is the way, truth and life (John 14:6) and were clearly led by the Spirit of truth (1 John 4:1-6), who guides all soft-hearted believers away from Satanic deception and fleshly concerns and into new life (John 6:63, Gal. 5:16-17). Those who overcame understood prophecy. They knew the scriptures and interpreted the times they were living in by the Spirit of God in them. Will you and I be one of them? Will the Son of Man find faith on Earth when He returns (Luke 18:8)?

The need for a Godly balance in Worship Services

Getting back to 1 Corinthians 14, Paul emphasises the need

for Godly order in church services - in the worship, prayer, prophesying and so on, because "God is not a God of confusion but of peace." (verses 33 and 40). I heard recently of youth event where the leader said that worship could be as messy <u>as people like it</u>, so long as the focus remained on God, yet Paul makes it clear that it should not be messy, but should instead be reverent to God through orderliness - hence the phrase: 'the order of service'. Though we shouldn't get so orderly that the Spirit is quenched and there's no joy, we should retain a Biblical standard of peace and order. We need balance. The Word and the Spirit bring all things into harmony.

The first two commandments show that our worship to God should be done in a proper way and not done in a way we like it. Those two commandments aren't just about not worshipping other gods and idols, but they are also about not having a wrong, (human) kind of worship to God. Again, this all boils down to the need to have the Holy Spirit, who is there to inspire and lead us into all truth and remind us of the truth of Jesus.

Jesus said:

...true worshippers will worship the Father in spirit and truth, for the Father is seeking such people to worship him. God is spirit, and those who worship him must worship in spirit and truth.

John 4:23-24

I see today that a lot of "charismatic" churches are getting drawn into worldly ways of worshipping God, where the worship times are more like an evening at a noisy nightclub with booming music, flashing lights, waving of phones, whooping and all the rest. There used to be a difference between going to church and going to a nightclub. We must keep them separate and never lose our reverential fear of the Lord. We shouldn't just copy others to draw more people in, but we must stand out from the crowd, which is the greatest witness to Christ out Lord!

Conclusion

The gift of tongues, the interpretation of them and the gift of prophecy are just some of the many, many gifts which the Spirit freely gives to believers to encourage others out of their helplessness, sorrow, pain, loss, bitterness, rejection and all other weaknesses that Satan tries to load people down with.

As with Jesus, the Spirit through His empowering nature, anoints us "to comfort all who mourn...provide for those who grieve...to bestow on them a crown of beauty instead of ashes, the oil of joy instead of mourning, and a garment of praise instead of a spirit of despair." (Study: Isa. 61, Luke 4:14-21, 2 Cor. 1:21-22).

Ultimately, the Holy Spirit with the fruit and gifts He brings change us into a much more loving, peaceful, joyful and useful people and they can also bring us to an ever-deepening relationship with God. They also help us align ourselves into God's will and make us more like Jesus. I believe we must always remember that Paul centres his words to the Corinthians with a teaching on love. He ends chapter 12 with the words "I will show you a still more excellent way" and then launches into his renowned words on love, found in the next chapter:

> If I speak in the tongues of men and of angels, but have not love, I am a noisy gong or a clanging cymbal. And if I have prophetic powers, and understand all mysteries and all knowledge, and if I have all faith, so as to remove mountains, but have not love, I am

nothing. If I give away all I have, and if I deliver up my body to be burned, but have not love, I gain nothing.

1 Corinthians 13:1-3

We must surely be believers who love, and place that above all the gifts. Jesus said that the world cannot accept His Spirit (John 14:17) and Paul says that the things of the Spirit appear as foolishness to man (1 Cor. 2:14), but as followers of Christ and believers in His Word we should receive more of His Spirit if we want to impact the world for Him. There are those who mock Christianity because of the gifts - especially the gift of tongues and there are members of various denominations who do not believe in them, even though they are Biblical and are good for all believers.

For example, I have come emphasised with many Charismatic Catholics who themselves have been sadly viewed with scepticism by their more traditional Catholic counterparts. I remember being told by two such traditionalists that it was dangerous for me to follow the Spirit and sinful for me not to pray to Mary! I hate to break it to the anti-Charismatic Catholics who attach such piety and seriousness to Mary and the saints so much, when in fact Mary and the first saints received the gift of tongues at Pentecost (Acts 1:14; 2:1-4)! They were Charismatic Christians!

In another way, I can express concern regarding some Charismatics - especially those from the more traditional backgrounds, who perhaps haven't had enough Biblical teaching about the gifts and have instead been fed a lot of ritual and legalism. When they receive the gifts of the Spirit they sometimes go somewhat hyper due to never having that balanced grounding in the Word.

Towards the end of His ministry, Jesus shared three consecutive Kingdom parables about the blessings we will or won't receive based on how we used the gifts God gave us (see: Matt. 25). The second of the three parables deals with how people use their 'talents' - as in wages rather than abilities. Even so, the word could easily apply to abilities or gifts. Please read the parable found in verse 13-30 of that chapter.

The Amplified Version renders Christ's conclusion to the story as:

> For to everyone who has [and values his blessings and gifts from God, and has used them wisely], more will be given, and [he will be richly supplied so that] he will have an abundance; but from the one who does not have [because he has ignored or disregarded his blessings and gifts from God], even what he does have will be taken away. And throw out the worthless servant into the outer darkness; in that place [of grief and torment] there will be weeping [over sorrow and pain] and grinding of teeth [over distress and anger].

> Matthew 25:29-30

It is a sobering reminder to all believers (including me) not to waste that which has been given freely. Why not patiently ask God to enhance the gifts you already have, show you ways to use them more and receive new ones if you are ready? Keep finding new ways to use them. God will anoint you more as you grow in Him and bless others through your talents, gifts and abilities.

Let us glean from Christ and lean on Christ!

6.

THE DEEPER THEOLOGY OF THE SPIRIT

"The history of revelation is still continuing...the canon is complete, but revelation is still flowing from it - because it's living. The Holy Spirit is alive...There's light and truth still to break out from its pages by the Holy Spirit [who] leads us into new things...[which] will always have a precedent in the scriptures."

Paul Miller, 2014

As with any fundamental Christian subject, there are always questions and areas that people like to discuss further to increase their knowledge and understanding. So, in this chapter, I want to discuss more topics and aspects already touched on in this book in more detail. In doing so I will delve more into the Old Testament for the roots of our belief in God the Holy Spirit.

Cessationism vs Continuationism

It would be absolutely no surprise to any reader of this book that I believe that the Holy Spirit is still empowering believers with the same spiritual gifts that the first Christians possessed 2,000 years ago. However, there are Christians out there who firmly believe or at least doubt that the Spirit works in the ways He did in New Testament times.

This belief I am referring to is known as 'cessationism'. It asserts that the gifts of the Spirit or at least some of them ceased with the death of the early apostles and ending of the Biblical canon. Cessationists call that time 'the Apostolic age' and state that it is long over. In other words, the gifts given at Pentecost were just to kick start the church, to empower the early believers to radically spread the Gospel and to inspire the writings of the New Testament. Once the last remaining disciple - John had completed the concluding book of the Bible - Revelation, around AD90 and died soon after, that was also the death of the gifts as well. Divine written revelation was over.

So, with the exception of the work of the Spirit regarding a person's salvation (and maybe with some spiritual gifts), there is now no more supernatural intervention or revelation from the Spirit to God's people.

Cessationists believe that God has given us all the revelation we need in the canon of scripture. Seen as many of the spiritual gifts are revelatory in nature (such as prophecy, tongues, interpretation, words of wisdom and knowledge etc.), proponents of this view believe that at least those gifts, if not all of them are no longer given by the Holy Spirit anymore. They would state that prophesies are no longer given through people and that you cannot receive the gifts of tongues anymore either. Christians who claim to prophesy now or speak in tongues are false or misguided somehow, i.e. they have just learnt to babble certain words.

Cessationists historically tend to come from the Evangelical wing of the church (although there are many exceptions), whereas 'Continuationists' tend to be amongst the Charismatic Christians (the clue is in the name). Pentecostals are probably the most well-known group of Charismatics. They believe we are still living in the days of Pentecost. However, there are Christians from all denominations who believe in the continuing gifts of the Spirit.

Members of the older, traditional circles such as the Orthodox, Catholic and Anglican communions contain a mix of Charismatics, Cessationists and those who simply haven't been taught about the gifts or 'charisms' of the Holy Spirit. I remember my R.E. teacher saying that we cannot perform miracles or heal people like the early disciples did. I believe she said that out of a lack of knowledge and understanding of the Word, rather than from a consciously cessationist viewpoint.

This cessationist view has its roots in dispensational thinking - which is the belief that the whole of human history has been divinely divided up into several 'dispensations' (I encourage you to look them up). These are periods of time that God has created where He tests man in different ways and provides different abilities during those times. They see the Apostolic age of the early disciples has having the gifts of the Spirit as the abilities given for that period. Then from the completion of the Bible, God gave a period which we are living in now - a timeframe where we just have the completed canon of scripture.

So, this dispensational / cessationist view is simply that what happened in the New Testament should not be expected to happen now, for example yes, we can pray for the sick to be healed, but we should not attempt to lay hands on the sick as Jesus and the early disciples did.

I find it impossible to accept the cessationist arguments because:

- there is a distinct lack of the Biblical evidence to support the belief that the Holy Spirit would stop equipping people with gifts after a certain point - when you read the New Testament through, there is nothing to suggest this.

- of mine and other people's experiences of the gifts being given and used today.

- it would not be in God's character to remove those gifts for later generations. Why are we different that those of the early church? Are we not followers of Christ as well who need the gifts which empowered the first Christians? Are we not part of the same church that was began by the outpouring of the Spirit at Pentecost?

- I don't recognise the dispensational divisions - I just see the Old Testament period - beginning with Adam and the New Testament period - beginning with the New Adam. Indeed, the last days began with Jesus (Heb. 1:1-2) and prophecies relating to that period are yet to come to fruition.

Let us go deeper. Paul's letter to the Ephesian church contains one of the aforementioned 'gift lists' found in scripture:

> So Christ himself gave the <u>apostles, the prophets, the evangelists, the pastors and teachers, to equip his people</u> for works of service, so that the body of Christ may be <u>built up until we all reach unity in the faith</u> and in the <u>knowledge</u> of the Son of God and become <u>mature</u>, attaining to <u>the whole measure</u> of the fullness of Christ.

> Ephesians 4:12-13

I would say that passage gives some clear evidence that the gifts have not stopped being distributed:

- We read that "Christ himself [them] gave" those gifts to His believers and Christ Himself said "whoever believes in me will do the works I have been doing, and they will do even greater things than these." (John 14:12). So, how could we do His work and even greater works than Him without the gifts He had?

- A typical cessationist would attend a church where there are evangelists, pastors (or a pastor) and teachers, yet they somehow dismiss the notion of still having apostles and prophets, because Apostolic age and the prophetic Biblical canon is over. Yet, why would God remove one or more of the ministries / gifts required to equip and build up the body? Do we not still need building up?

- Cessationists (such as well-known American Pastor - John MacArthur) rightly say that prophecies are revelations from God to man, but wrongly say that prophecy ended with the completion of divine revelation, namely with the last book of the Bible - Revelation and when those first disciples died. MacArthur and many others like him state that only prophecies within the Biblical canon and timeframe count. Yet, Enoch who lived at least 1,500 years before the Bible began to be written prophesied the return of the Lord! It is Jude who refers to this and he uses extra-Biblical material to support it (see: Jude 0:14)!

- Paul says above that the five-fold ministry is needed to equip and build up the body and until we reach perfect knowledge, a complete maturity and unity in the fullness of Christ. That has not been achieved in the 2,000-year history of the church and we are still far from reaching that - therefore we still need and have the gifts. Surely Paul is referring to the day when Christ returns - it is only then all things will be perfect and complete.

- The Prophet Joel predicted that "in the last days" God's believers would prophesy and that God would show signs and wonders in the Heavens before the great and terrible day of the Lord (the Second Coming). We are still living "in the last days" and there is no hint that God would remove the gift of prophecy, nor the other gifts which came as the fulfilment of that prophecy at Pentecost (Acts 2). In a sense, Joel's prophecy has not yet been completely fulfilled - as those signs he spoke have not all occurred yet. We are indeed still living in a time of gifts being given by the Spirit and awaiting more signs and wonders in the heavens that he predicted (see: Joel 2:28-32).

A passage often used by Cessationist thinkers to justify their view is from this well-known passage from Paul:

Love never fails. But where there are prophecies, they will cease; where there are tongues, they will be stilled; where there is knowledge, it will pass away. For we know in part and we prophesy in part, but when completeness comes, what is in part disappears... For now we see only a reflection as in a mirror; then we shall see face to face. Now I know in part; then I shall know fully, even as I am fully known.

1 Corinthians 13:8-10, 12

Paul is explaining to us that in our limited minds and in this imperfect world we do not see or know everything about God, the

Bible and the future, therefore speaking tongues and prophecies only reveal partial knowledge about God. However, much like the Ephesian passage above, Paul refers to the time of "completeness" when what is in part will disappear. It is not the completion of the dispensation, but the return of Jesus when we shall we Jesus face to face in all His fullness and not just "in part".

So, the gifts will only cease when Christ returns, because when we are with Him, we'll know everything, for "we shall be like him, for we shall see him as he is" (1 John 3:2). We won't need the gifts anymore, because they'll be no more spiritual goals or battles or enemies to conquer through prophesying, evangelising and fighting the good fight etc. All that was prophesied in the Bible will have been fulfilled and so all these gifts will be unnecessary. Only faith, hope and love will remain for all eternity (1 Cor. 13:13).

Back in Ephesians, Paul also says that when Christ ascended into Heaven He then "gave gifts to His people" - which, as we know was done through the outpouring of His Spirit at Pentecost (Eph. 4:8). Jesus did that so we would all be spiritually equipped with the gifts until the day when He returns. Why would God remove those very gifts just a few decades after Pentecost as cessationists claim? It is when Christ descends back from Heaven when will no longer need the gifts of the Spirit. Until then we are in bodies which are wasting away and have been "given us the Spirit as a deposit, guaranteeing what is to come." (2 Cor. 5:5).

To summarise, here is the sequence of events in church history:

Christ's ascension - giving of spiritual gifts at the birth of
the church

Christ's return - no need for spiritual gifts for the church

Many cessationists who witness people speaking in tongues
say it's from the Devil. That is a potentially dangerous position, as it
could be an example of committing the unforgiveable sin, which I
will discuss further on in this chapter.

The aforementioned cessationist Pastor John MacArthur has
heavily criticised some Charismatic groups, stating that their church
services and conferences are being influenced by the demonic. He
claims that the followers of these movements are being deceived
into thinking it's the work of the Holy Spirit, when really it is the
Devil who is at work. Surely such an assertion is rather flawed,
because he accepts that manifestations of unholy spirits are still
occurring today, yet does not accept that the manifestations of the
Holy Spirit are (John MacArthur - Strange Fire Conference -
Kundalini Spirit, 2014).

Now, despite my objections to what he is saying, I do accept
that there are a growing number of 'Christians' who are getting
hyped up in 'Charismania'. I believe many are potentially being led
astray by lying, deceiving spirits. The Bible warned this would
happen to many people in the last days (2 Cor. 14:1-15, 2 Tim. 4:3,
1 John 4:1-6). I am not afraid to join MacArthur in suggesting that
the work of the enemy is present in *some* movements because the
teachings and practices of those movements are clearly far from

Biblical, yet what bothers me is when MacArthur and alike brand all spiritual manifestations as being of the Devil or at least of the flesh. That is when it is dangerous and also in contradiction to his cessationist views.

As I said earlier, cessationists tend to come from Evangelical churches. They usually take the Word very seriously - so seriously that I think it has taken the place of the Spirit. Such a position leads to legalism to the extent that the fire of the Spirit is quenched. I have heard a number of people state that some evangelical churches can be a little cold and cerebral in nature. In fact, some Evangelical churches do believe in the gifts to a degree, but will often just teach that people should only wait on God to give them, yet Paul tells us to "earnestly seek" the gifts of the Spirit for ourselves. He also states that we should not lack the spiritual gifts (1 Cor. 1:6-7; 12:31; 14:1, 12).

Cessationists will often argue that there is little or no evidence for the continuance of the gifts through the centuries of church history, yet there have been many revivals throughout the years. Such occurrences have given rise to people being empowered with amazing spiritual gifts - namely the abilities to share faith, mercy and hospitality to unbelievers.

Consider these examples:

- The Quaker movement - beginning in the mid-17th century was born out of a desire to be more led by the Spirit and this in turn led to many successful businesses, banks and charities being started. Such institutions are still with us today: think of Rowntree's, Cadbury's, John Lewis, Clarks shoes, Sony, Lloyds Bank, Barclay's, Oxfam, Amnesty International and Greenpeace to name but a few. The Quakers made sure they built these institutions with godly principles, which is why I believe they have succeeded for so long (Wikipedia. 2016).

- The Evangelical Revival of the 18th century, involving John Newton was a clear move of God's Spirit, who empowered many with His gifts. This in part inspired MP William Wilberforce to successfully get slavery abolished and to set up charities for children and also for animals - such as the RSPCA (Wikipedia, 2016).

- The Wesleyan Revival of the latter half of the 18th century led to an even greater outpouring of God's gifts and to many Methodists being empowered to reach out to their communities. Indeed, John Wesley lamented the lack of spiritual gifts through the centuries of Christendom and clearly believed in them himself (Robert G. Jr Tuttle). In relation to this, I once heard of a preacher who was asked to speak at a Methodist church in the Midlands on Pentecost Sunday some years ago. He was told he could speak on anything so long as he didn't mention the Holy Spirit! Though this is not true of some Methodist churches, there is clearly a need for a spiritual renewal in that church along with many other denominations.

- More recent revivals of the 20th century in all four nations of the UK and of course not forgetting the Charismatic renewal of the 1960's and 70's have all led to waves of people experiencing healing and miracles. Many have come to salvation and also to a fresh, renewed passion for the Lord and to fulfilling the Great Commission.

- UK Christian organisations such as *The World Prayer Centre*, *Redeeming Our Communities* (ROC), *HOPE, Open Doors* and *Care for the Family* all have Spirit-filled leadership teams. They are carrying on the amazing outreach work of the first Christians by using the Spirit-given gifts here and now. Without those gifts they would not nearly be as effective in reaching the lost and the persecuted.

- Billy Graham (1919-2018), preached the Gospel to more people than anyone in history believed that the continuing work of the Spirit had brought more people to Christ than anyone else through his 60-year evangelistic ministry. His son, Franklin continues his amazing work across the globe.

- David Pawson (1930-), has long advocated the gifts of the Spirit and like Graham, has reached the world for the Gospel with his Spirit-led Bible teachings.

All these moves of God's Spirit are needed at the time they were given. Out of the worst situations and in the most darkened communities God wants to bring His light. It comes about due to persistent, faithful prayer and not just by waiting alone or by cowering away. Each one led to a greater love for God, His Word and for people. Jesus said it would be through love that people will tell we are His followers (John 13:34-35). Only by our openness to

His Spirit who wants to plant the seed of love and empower us with spiritual gifts in all of us will we see mighty changes in our nation, community, family and in our own individual lives.

Much of what happened at those revivals along with the countless others is consistent with the Bible's teaching on the gifts of the Spirit and who and what they are for. Consider these words:

> <u>Now to each one</u> the manifestation of the Spirit is given for the common good...the one who prophesies speaks to people for their strengthening, encouraging and comfort. What then shall we say, brothers and sisters? When you come together, each of you has a hymn, or a word of instruction, a revelation, a tongue or an interpretation. Everything must be done so that the church may be built up. Concerning...salvation, the prophets...spoke of the grace that was to come to you...It was revealed to them that <u>they were not serving themselves but you</u>, when they spoke of the things that have now been told you by those who have preached the gospel to you by the Holy Spirit sent from heaven.

1 Corinthians 12:7; 14:3, 26, 1 Peter 1:10-12

To the people who are undecided about the gifts and to those who are convinced that the gifts have ceased long ago, I would challenge them to really ask God to reveal the truth of the matter. The Bereans believers examined the scriptures daily to see whether Paul's teachings were of God. They received the promised Spirit that he spoke of because he taught the truth and they as with all people need the Holy Spirit to equip and empower them through the gifts He freely gives.

Many of the Jews wanted a relationship with God the Father, but without Jesus, and many Christians today only want to walk about God the Father and God the Son, but without the Spirit of God. We need to know God in all His fullness and receive all that He has to offer us according to His Word and according to His Spirit.

The Three Great Feasts

A potentially helpful way of looking at the need to believe and receive the fullness of God in one's life is to explore the cycle of the Church calendar and compare it to a person's life.

In the traditional churches (i.e. Catholic, Anglican and Orthodox) along with a number of others, the Church calendar begins on the first Sunday of Advent (usually end of November or early December) and takes the faithful on a journey throughout the next 12 months.

I believe that these three main Christian seasons of Advent to Christmas, Lent to Easter and Ascension to Pentecost formed from the New Testament are fulfilments of the three great pilgrimage feasts of the Jewish calendar established by God Himself in the Old Testament. They correspond to the Feast of Tabernacles, the Feast of Passover and the Feast of Weeks (see: Exod. 23:14-19).

These three Christians feasts can represent a journey that God wants to take in us and with us. They relate to God as Father, Son and Spirit.

JEWISH SEASON / FEAST	CHRISTIAN SEASON / FEAST
At Sukkoth / the Feast of Tabernacles (or Booths) the Jews would build shelters to symbolise God's protection and light may lights to symbolise His glory, truth and purity. The Hebrew word Sukkoth can be translated as 'stable'.	During Advent and Christmas, we celebrate the birth of Jesus who was born in an animal's stable, who "became flesh and tabernacled with us". He was "the light of the world", who's arrival was announced by a bright shining star and a host of startlingly radiant angels.
At Pesach / Passover – a Lamb was sacrificed to cover the sins of the Jewish. They remembered how God delivered them from the Angel of Death and from captivity. They crossed from death into life.	During Lent and Easter, we remember the Lamb of God who was slain for our sins and those of the whole world. He was raised back to life for our salvation and to deliver us from our captivity in sin.
At Shavuot / the Feast of Weeks – the Jews celebrate the giving of the Law to Moses on Mount Sinai. They received the Word of the Lord.	In the seven weeks between Easter and Pentecost, (including the Ascension) we remember how the early Christians gathered together following Christ's ascent from Mount Zion to receive the promised Holy Spirit.

Pentecost and the Fulfilment of Prophecy

In the Old Testament, it was prophesied that a mighty day would come when all believers would be filled and empowered with God's Spirit and that many wondrous signs would follow (Joel 2). Up until the fulfilment in Pentecost c. 30 AD, the Holy Spirit only filled or empowered a few select holy people, such as the prophets (see: 1 Pet. 1:10-12). Here are some more examples of pre-Pentecost (Acts 2) people who were influenced, filled or overshadowed by the Holy Spirit for a time and even for their entire lives:

- Joseph (Gen. 41:38)
- Aaron, his sons and priests were anointed (Exod. 28:41, Num. 3:3 etc)
- Bezalel (Exod. 31:3; 35:31)
- Moses and the 70 Israelite elders (Num. 11:16-29)
- Balaam (Num. 24:2)
- Joshua (Num. 27:18, Deut. 34:9)
- Othniel (Jud. 3:9-10)
- Gideon (Jud. 6:34)
- Jephthah (Jud. 11:29)
- Samson (Jud. 13:24-25; 14:6, 19; 15:14)
- Saul (1 Sam. 10:6-11; 19:23)
- Saul's army (1 Sam. 19:20)

- David (1 Sam. 16:13-14; 23:2, 1 Chr. 28:12, see also: Psa. 51:10-13)
- Obadiah (1 Ki. 18:22)
- Zedekiah (1 Ki. 22:24, 2 Chr. 18:23)
- Elijah and Elisha (2 Ki. 2:9, 13-15)
- Amasai (1 Chr. 12:18)
- Azariah (2 Chr. 15:1)
- Jahaziel (2 Chr. 20:14)
- Zechariah (2 Chr. 24:20)
- Isaiah (Isa. 61:1-3) - Jesus later applied this to Himself.
- Ezekiel (Ezek. 2:1-3) - Some translations refer to a wind coming into Him and some say the Spirit coming into Him. There are so many examples of the Spirit doing amazing things through Ezekiel, it would be too long a list.
- Daniel (see: Dan. 4- 5) - all references to this are from pagans who incorrectly say he has "the spirit of the holy gods", instead of the Holy Spirit of God.
- Micah (Mic. 3:8)
- Mary (Luke 1:35)
- Elizabeth (Luke 1:41)
- Zechariah (Luke 1:67)
- John the Baptist (Luke 1:15; 80) - He prophesied the outpouring of the Spirit and was Spirit-filled before he was even born!
- Simeon (Luke 2:25-27)

There must have been many more unrecorded examples in Biblical times too, but never to all believers before Pentecost, for as John pointed out in his Gospel, "for as yet the Spirit had not been given because Jesus was not yet glorified." (John 7:39). Jesus had to clear the way for the Holy Spirit to come in greater fullness by taking on Himself all the unholiness of our sins and then being glorified through His resurrection and ascension back to the right hand of the Father.

The Book of Joel holds the most detailed prophecy. At the Pentecost when the Spirit came down, Peter stands up to address the believers gathered and says,

> …this was spoken by the prophet Joel: <u>In the last days</u>, God says, I will pour out my Spirit on <u>all</u> people. Your sons and daughters will prophesy, your young men will see visions, your old men will dream dreams. Even on my servants, both men and women, <u>I will pour out my Spirit in those days</u>, and they will prophesy. I will show wonders in the heavens above and signs on the earth below, blood and fire and billows of smoke. The sun will be turned to darkness and the moon to blood before the coming of the great and glorious day of the Lord. And <u>everyone who calls on the name of the Lord will be saved</u>.

See: Acts 2:14-21 and Joel 2:28-32

This passage shows that the Holy Spirit was prophesied as being poured out in a period of human history called "the last days" or "the latter time". The Spirit was poured out almost 2,000 years ago, meaning the last days began sometime before then. In addition, we are still in that period, because not everything in that prophecy has been fulfilled yet.

Despite this, Peter felt the need to quote it all. On some level he knew the people of God had entered a time when these things would occur. So, when did the last days begin? The opening words of the Book of Hebrews make it clear. The writer states that in the past God spoke to us through His prophets, but now "in these last days he has spoken to us by his Son" (see: Heb. 1:1-2). So, the First Coming of Christ ushered in a new era - the last days / the Apostolic age / the Church age / the Kingdom age. (see also: 1 Pet. 1:3-5).

The passage above from Acts (quoting Joel) also show that there's a dividing line. We either receive the Lord's Holy Spirit and call on the name of the Lord or we follow our own evil desires and promote ourselves. The early Babylonians who built the Tower of Babel were like the latter. Genesis 11:1-9 tells the story:

> Now the whole world had <u>one language and a common speech</u>. As people moved eastward, they found a plain in Shinar and settled there. They said to each other... 'Come, let us build ourselves a city, with a tower that reaches to the heavens, <u>so that we may make a name for ourselves</u>; otherwise we will be scattered over the face of the whole earth.' But the Lord came down to see the city and the tower the people were building. The Lord said, 'If as one people speaking the same language they have begun to do this, then nothing they plan to do will be impossible for them. Come, <u>let us</u> go down and confuse their language so they will not understand each other.' So the Lord scattered them from there over all the earth, and they stopped building the city. That is why it was called Babel — because there the Lord

confused the language of the whole world.[1] From there the Lord scattered them over the face of the whole earth.

Here is a table showing how Pentecost is a reversal of what happened in Babel:

GENESIS 11 UNSPIRITUAL UNBELIEVERS	ACTS 2 SPIRIT-FILLED BELIEVERS
Everyone tried to form a false unity in rebellion of God's first ever command to spread, multiply and fill the Earth.	Everyone waited in unity in obedience to God and Christ's command.
They all spoke the same language, but God said, "let us" (because He is Father, Son and Spirit) go down to confuse their language.	They all spoke the same language and God came down to give them new spiritual language – the gift of tongues.
Man's false kingdom created through his own fleshly efforts.	God's church and kingdom was established by His Spirit.
They said they wanted to make a name for themselves to challenge God.	Peter said that anyone who calls upon the name of the Lord will be saved.

---

[1] The origin of the word 'Babel' is commonly thought to be connected to the words 'baby' and 'babble'.

The Babel / Babylonian system has always opposed God and His people right the way through the scriptures. The Books of Daniel, Isaiah, Ezekiel and Revelation draw particular attention to this.

What happened at that Pentecost really does represent God's Spirit coming down to us, purifying us and empowering us. To the Jews, Pentecost (or Shavuot) was a celebration of the Law. It commemorates God giving Moses the Ten Commandments on Mount Sinai. It became known as the Feast of Weeks as the event occurred seven weeks after the Passover, when the Jews were liberated from Egypt. We celebrate Pentecost seven weeks after Easter Sunday.

This Feast was originally a celebration of the giving of God's commands and over time it became a celebration of the giving of God's Word (see: Ex. 23, 32-34). So, the Christian believers gather for this great Feast. God sending His Spirit at this celebration of His Word is again bringing the Spirit and the Word together.

Pentecost remembers the time when Moses comes down the mountain with the Ten Commandments and furiously throws them down because he sees the impatient Jews worshipping an idol – the Golden Calf (Exod. 32). As a judgment on the idolaters, Moses destroys the idol with fire and God allows 3,000 idolaters to be killed. Now zoom forward to Pentecost Sunday in Acts 2 - God sends down His fire on the patient, believers to empower them. Peter preaches and we read that 3,000 people were saved that day. It is a revival of reversal. Instead of 3,000 sermons with only one conversion, there is one Spirit-empowered sermon preached and 3,000 are converted!

Back in Exodus 32, Moses sees how the Israelites had become wild and angrily asks Aaron why he allowed the people to give into to idolatry and Aaron says that "You know how prone these people are to evil" (verse 22). This is why God eventually sends us His Holy Spirit because we so easily give in to sin. Jesus said the Holy Spirit would convict us of our wrongdoing and that's why the world cannot receive Him because the world wants to carry on following their own carnal, fleshly desires.

Paul says in Galatians, in Ephesians, Romans and elsewhere that the things of the flesh (our own selfish desires) are in opposition to the things of the Spirit. That's why we need the infilling of the Spirit to drive out the evil within us. We can't be like Jesus with His Spirit. He was perfect and sinless, we are not. But as Paul also says, the Holy Spirit is the Spirit of Christ who must live in us (Rom. 8:9). Therefore, we need an emersion of His Holy Spirit.

So, Pentecost occurs seven weeks after Passover which was when Jesus died as the final sacrificial lamb to take away all the sins of the world for those who would accept that (John 1:29; 1 John 1:7-9). When He breathed His last on the cross, we read that the temple curtain that separated people from the holy of holies was torn in two (Mark 15:38). This symbolises how Jesus reconciled man back to God for those who believe. Behind the holy of holies was God's presence - His Spirit. 50 days later the Spirit was poured out on all believers waiting at the Temple. His Spirit was given for all and not just for some (Acts 2:16-18).

The Temple of the Holy Spirit

It is almost universally assumed that the Holy Spirit fell on the believers in 'the Upper Room' (the Cenacle), as that was the room they used for the Last Supper (Mark 14:15) and also for when they gathered together in Acts 1 (see: verse 13). When the Holy Spirit does come in Acts 2, we read about "the whole house in which they were sitting" (verse 2). The 'house' or 'house of prayer' was actually a term for the Temple (2 Chr. 5:13, Matt. 21:13, Acts 15:15-16, 1 Pet. 2:4-6). Also, the very last verse of Luke says that the after Jesus ascended back to Heaven the disciples "stayed continually at the temple, praising God" (Luke 24:53).

Consider these other points about the Temple:

- could take 120+ people, whereas the upper room probably couldn't (Acts 1:15)

- was the place Jews gathered for the major feasts of their religious calendar, including Pentecost (Festival of Weeks) was celebrated every year (Deut. 16:11; 26:1-4).

- was where the disciples continued to meet before and after Pentecost (Luke 24:53, Acts 2:46).

- is (as I say) referred to as 'the house' or 'the house of God / the Lord' (1 Kings 6-10, Psa. 122, Matt. 21:12-13, Heb. 10:21-22) and when addressing the gathering crowds at Pentecost, Peter calls on the people of 'the house of Israel' to turn to Christ, implying that he is addressing people gathered at the Temple (the House) for the Festival (Acts 2:36)

- was where God's Spirit (His Presence) dwelt until the curtain was torn in two (Psa. 26:8, Matt. 12:1-8; 27:51) thanks to Jesus' death bridging the gap man made through sin against God, so when the Spirit came down, it filled <u>the whole temple</u> so no one was restricted anymore - "I will pour out my Spirit on <u>all</u> flesh" (Acts 2:16-17. See also: Heb. 9-10)

We are now the temple of the Holy Spirit (Rom. 8:9, 1 Cor. 3:16, 1 Pet. 2:4-6). God is holy; man is not because of his sin, so God can't dwell with man, therefore God's Son has to take the sin of the world. Adam brought sin into the world, so Jesus came as the New Adam (1 Cor. 15:45). When we accept what Jesus did for us, we are saved, purified from sin, so therefore for God's Spirit (His Presence) can come into us, but we also need the baptism that the early believers experienced.

> Do you not know that your bodies are temples of the Holy Spirit, who is in you, whom you have received from God? You are not your own; you were bought at a price. Therefore honour God with your bodies.
>
> 1 Corinthians 6:19-20

Paul calls our bodies "the temple of the Holy Spirit", because we have the Spirit of Jesus dwelling in us (1 Cor. 3:16; 6:19), just as God's Spirit dwelt in the Temple in Jerusalem (1 Kings 8). When the Temple is rebuilt, God's Spirit comes again (Ezra 6:12, see also: Matt. 23:21). Ezra lived in a time of restoration for the Jews who come out of exile and back to their spiritual homeland. They return to the holy laws of God and realise how far they had fallen from God, yet they still believed in Him. As one reads Nehemiah and Ezra, we see a return of the Word and of the Spirit in the hearts of God's people. Many Christians today need this in their lives.

The return to God's Word, the re-inhabiting of His Spirit and the restoration of the Temple which happened in Ezra and Nehemiah's day can apply to the story of one's life. They also helped to rebuild the walls of Jerusalem. In our lives, our walls maybe a little damaged in part due to knowingly or unknowingly allowing sin to the enter through a lack of good, godly boundaries. In Jerusalem's glory days, King Solomon once said: "Like a city whose walls are broken through is a person who lacks self-control." (Prov. 25:28).

In the original Temple, King David had watchman standing guard at the North, South, East and West gate of the Holy Temple (1 Chr. 26). As Temples of God's <u>Holy</u> Spirit, we too must "guard [our] hearts and [our] minds in Christ Jesus" from all unholiness which tries to corrupt us (Phil. 4:7, see also: Prov. 4:23). We get attacked on all sides and therefore, we must not let the Devil gain a place in our heart or mind - the Temple. God has given us weapons to fight the enemy from entering, including our spiritual eyes, ears and mouth. Even love is a weapon (see: Eph. 4:17-32; 5:1-20 and 6:10-18).

It may be difficult for many to accept that a person can have the presence of God dwelling inside them and for that person to also have demonic spirits residing there too. Yet, I have come across clearly genuine Christians who had the Spirit of God in them and with them and yet also had evil spirits which were driven out of them. It is like how the Temple had the presence (the Spirit) of God residing in the Holy of Holies (the inner part of the Temple) and also at times in Israel's history, the Temple had prostitutes and money changers and all sorts of ungodly practices going on in the outer parts. In our spirit, the Holy Spirit dwells, but in our soul evil spirits can also dwell and must be driven out.

Conscience

Having the <u>Holy</u> Spirit indwelling us is quite an amazing thing to say the very least. It does however mean that the holiness of God is always present and therefore can clash with the unholiness that is also in us. The word 'holy' is 'Sanctus' in Latin and is where we get the word 'saint' and 'sanctify', with all the derivatives thereof.

The Apostle Peter opens his first epistle with a few Trinitarian words acknowledging "the sanctification of the Spirit" in a believer's life. In fact, the entire first chapter of his epistle especially centres on the call to holiness. It is quite clear that to "be holy, for [God is] holy" is impossible without the leading and the guiding of the indwelling Spirit (see: 1 Pet. 1).

The Holy Spirit of God sanctifies us in our Christian walk, which means that as we glean and lean on Christ, we are made ever more holy. That's is sanctification. Christ's death and resurrection brought sanctification to our souls and made a way for us to approach the holy Father and return to Him one day as completely renewed, sanctified, perfect people (Rom. 6, 1 Cor. 6:11, Heb. 2:11; 4;15-16; 10:10, Rev. 22). It is the Holy Spirit's role to continually work in us and ready us for the life to come.

God has given every man and woman a conscience - a moral sense of right and wrong, which helps them govern their decisions (Rom. 2:5). It is a faculty of the human spirit. Depending on our upbringing and what we are exposed to, that conscience is either strengthened or weakened. Again, this is why we need the holiness of God's Spirit in and with us. He refines our conscience so that our thoughts, words and actions conform more to that of Christ's - so we become more holy. Many people act on conscience, but their conscience maybe seared or dulled to God's good moral standards (1 Tim. 4:1-2).

Paul states:

> God has revealed [many things] to us through the Spirit. For the Spirit searches everything, even the depths of God. For who knows a person's thoughts except the spirit of that person, which is in him? So also no one comprehends the thoughts of God except the Spirit of God. Now we have received not the spirit of the world, but the Spirit who is from God, that we might understand the things freely given us by God. And we impart this in words not taught by human wisdom but taught by the Spirit, interpreting spiritual truths to those who are spiritual. The natural person does not accept the things of the Spirit of God, for they are folly to him, and he is not able to understand them because they are spiritually discerned. The spiritual person judges all things, but is himself to be judged by no one. "For who has understood the mind of the Lord so as to instruct him?" But we have the mind of Christ.

1 Corinthians 2:10-16

Knowing and living this brings blessing through closer relationship with our Heavenly Father and makes us much more effective in spreading the Gospel of Christ.

I have noticed how the Spirit of God is interested in many of the smaller things of life. Many times, I have felt a prompt that doesn't seem to have come from me, but from God. In a conversation with someone I have had this spiritual sense not to say what just popped in my head, as it is somehow wrong, sinful or unhelpful to say. When I have disobeyed, it has led to an argument and / or an offence being caused. I have had to apologise and repent for not following what the Spirit was prompting me in my conscience. Paul says to let our good conscience before God block us from entering into "vain discussion" and arguments particularly with other Christians (see: 1 Tim. 1:3-7).

At other, times, I have been prompted *to* say something. It may be to share the Gospel or something of God in order that a seed might be sown in another's heart. Again, I have sometimes disobeyed this more times than I care to remember and no doubt it has been of a loss to the other person. Again, I have had to repent to God. Jesus actually said that when you are put on trial and are questioned for your faith to "not worry about how to defend yourselves or what to say. For at that time the Holy Spirit will teach you what you should say." (Luke 12:12).

God through the refining fire of His Spirit - thinks, speaks and acts through us more and more as we draw closer to the Father and the Son every day and in every way. A daily diet of personal prayer and study of the Word and regular diet of group prayer and study of the scriptures are the greatest ways to do this.

Paul says,

> The aim of our charge is love that issues from a pure heart and a good conscience and a sincere faith. Certain persons, by swerving from these, have wandered away into vain discussion, desiring to be teachers of the law, without understanding either what they are saying or the things about which they make confident assertions.

1 Timothy 1:5-7

We often do not sense the convicting prompts of the Spirit due to our hearts being a little dull, cold or hard (Heb. 3:7-15). There can be areas of our life which are tarnished by sin without us realising it. This is because we perhaps haven't grown up to the point of realising that yet. King David said in the Psalms that he repented of his "presumptuous sins" and humbly asked the Spirit not to leave him due to his transgressions (see: Psa. 19:13 and all of 51). I say, the more we draw close to Christ by His Spirit - the more we will know what is right and what is wrong in our thinking, our speaking and our acting.

Paul says in Romans 2 that on Judgment Day, a person's conscience will either accuse or excuse them. I remember Paul Miller stating how a person's conscience is like "an internal court" that weighs our choices and actions. Why not ask the Holy Spirit to inspire you to pray and read the Word more and to show you the areas you need to change which are conflicting with His convicting?

Blasphemy against the Spirit

The scripture makes it clear that we are not to grieve the Holy Spirit or quench His fire due to our sin (Eph. 4:30, 1 Thes. 5:19). If we do, we must repent. Some Christians knowingly, persistently and purposefully live a life of sin after coming to faith in God. If they do, they are "trampl[ing] the Son of God underfoot" who sanctifies each believer and are insulting "the Spirit of grace" who is there to lead the sinner out of sin (see: Heb. 10:22-31).

Notice, that the writer uses the word 'grace' as the main attribute of the Spirit there. God is so gracious to us even when we insult Him and He wants to draw us back through the wonder of His amazing grace. He is loving, merciful, gentle and kind.

Further than this, Peter warns about *blaspheming* Christ and *blaspheming* "the Spirit of glory" who rests on each believer (see: 1 Pet. 4:14-16 in NKJV). This relates back to some well-known words of warning from Christ Himself on this matter.

They are found in all three Synoptic Gospel's, but let's look at Matthew's account, who appears to give the most detailed account:

> "Therefore I say to you, every sin and blasphemy will be forgiven men, but the blasphemy against the Spirit <u>will not be forgiven men</u>. Anyone who speaks a word against the Son of Man, it will be forgiven him; but

whoever speaks against the Holy Spirit, it will not be forgiven him, either in this age or in the age to come.

Matthew 12:31-32
(see also: Mark 3:28-29 and Luke 12:10)

These words have doubtless caused many through the centuries to ponder as to what exactly He meant or even to worry as to whether they had committed this unforgiveable sin. The world's best-known evangelist - Billy Graham recounts in his book on the Holy Spirit about how his father had worried for years and years that he had committed this "unpardonable sin" (as it is also known) after hearing a sermon on the subject. He was convinced of it and it took a long time for him to realise he hadn't. How did he know that and that he would be saved from unquenchable fires? The fact that he was bothered about it! (Billy Graham, 1978 (1988).

If you feel a sense of guilt or a conviction in your heart about the fact that you *may* have blasphemed the Spirit of God, you can be assured that you haven't. Why? Because you almost certainly wouldn't be aware that you'd committed the unforgivable sin. You would be so far from God as to not know or care. In the vast majority of cases, only those who do not care about what they say about the Spirit are in danger of blaspheming the Spirit of glory and of grace.

If you have the Spirit infilling you, He will surely prevent you from this unless you of course fall away into deception or turn away into a life of sin (2 Tim. 2:12-13, Heb. 2:2-4). For as Paul says, "I want you to know that no one who is speaking by the Spirit of God says, "Jesus be cursed," and no one can say, "Jesus is Lord," except by the Holy Spirit." (1 Cor. 12:3).

The greater context of the Matthew scripture above shows that Jesus had been accused (or accursed, to use Paul's word) by some of the unbelieving Pharisees of drawing on the power of Satan rather than from Jehovah (see: Matt. 12:22-30). That I believe is what Jesus was referring to as an example of blaspheming the Holy Spirit.

I believe it is almost certainly only unbelievers who can commit such a sin and therefore forfeit their place in Heaven. It is the highest form of offence to say that the Holy Spirit is actually an unholy spirit of Satan himself. I would say that saying Satan is the Holy Spirit is possibly committing the same sin as well.

Indeed, the way to see whether someone is acting under the influence of the Holy Spirit or under the influence of an unholy spirit is to see what fruit they produce - as Jesus explains afterward speaking on this blasphemy (Matt. 12:33-45, see also: 1 John 4:1-5).

There are some related stories from the Bible which may classify as examples of blaspheming the Holy Spirit:

- in Genesis 6, we read of the people of Noah's day could only think, speak and act evil. God was grieved, insulted and blasphemed and said that His Spirit could no longer strive for so long with evil man anymore.

- and in Acts 7:51, the first Christian martyr - Stephen rebukes unbelieving Pharisees around him for being so "stiff-necked" as to "always resist the Holy Spirit" (see: Prov. 29:1). In both cases, man's unholiness was too great for God's Spirit of holiness to continue with them.

For us who believe, these stories and Christ's warning are reminders to remain in Him, which means He will remain in us and the Spirit of God will continue to strive within us (see: John 15:51-11, Rom. 8:1-17, Eph. 4:30, Heb. 10:26-39).

The author of 'From Witchcraft to Christ', Doreen Irving is an example of someone who can come from such an incredibly dark place to a place of knowing Jesus and being forgiven by Him. It appears that she did not blaspheme the Holy Spirit despite the Satanic activities they got involved in. I believe that story and many like it give hope to those who are concerned if they have committed the unforgiveable sin.

Those who accused Jesus and those who accused Stephen were the spiritual leaders of their day. They had the very Word of God given them and were part of God's Chosen People. They obviously knew enough about God and His Word so as to not blaspheme the Spirit *of* God. But perhaps that was the problem. They knew *about* God, but did not *know* God, just as Saul did before He came to Christ. If they knew God, they almost certainly would not blaspheme His Holy Spirit. After all, we must love God with <u>all</u> our heart, soul, mind and strength, love our neighbour and our enemy and love the truth - all four loves are conscious acts which will keep us from deception and destruction (see: Matt. 5:44, Luke 10:27 and 2 Thess. 2:10-13).

There are those who get sucked into occultism and witchcraft before realising what it is and how blasphemous it is, whereas there are those who do know what they are doing and will undoubtedly be blaspheming God as Father, Son and Spirit and will therefore forfeit their place in eternal glory with the saints of God.

John shares this towards the end of the Bible:

Blessed are those who wash their robes and do his commandments so that they may have the right to the tree of life and that they may enter the city by the gates. Outside are the dogs and sorcerers and the sexually immoral and murderers and idolaters, and everyone who loves and practises falsehood. "I, Jesus, have sent my angel to testify to you about these things for the churches. I am the root and the descendant of David, the bright morning star." The Spirit and the Bride say, "Come." And let the one who hears say, "Come." And let the one who is thirsty come; let the one who desires take the water of life without price.

Revelation 22:12-17

Notice, that passage applies only to those who seek the life God offers and join the Spirit in desiring the return of Christ. Outside are those who resisted His Spirit and through the vile sins they refused to repent of or that were so grievous they blocked their entry into Heaven.

After that passage comes a solemn warning not to add or take away from the book of Revelation (see: verses 18-19). Anyone who does, will also be prevented from eternal life with God. The Holy Spirit inspired the writing of Revelation, the prophecies therein and indeed the writing and prophecies in every book of the Bible (2 Tim. 3:16-17, 2 Peter 1:20-21, Rev. 2:11).

Therefore, if you add or take away the perfect truth which the Spirit has given, you may be adding dangerous lies or removing vital truths which could lead you astray and into Hell. It is an utter insult to the Spirit to alter the sacred Word which He inspired.

The Spirit of God is the presence of God (Psa. 139:7) and when people have felt this strongly through a powerful worship or prayer time (2 Chr. 5:13-14, Psa. 22:3) or even through near a death experience, there is absolutely no denying that it is the Spirit of the one true God - their Lord, Saviour and Creator. Therefore, if someone can stand there in that utter, astounding, wondrous presence of God and say it is Satan, they must be truly so evil and far from God as one can be. To say such an abominable thing is surely to commit the unpardonable blasphemy against the Spirit of God.

Those who accused Jesus - the Son of God that He was operating in the power of Satan were doing the same. They were literally standing in front of God and were accusing Him of cavorting with the Devil! That sort of sin and utter rejection of Christ is so deep and so painful that it us unforgiveable - even for God who forgives all sin. It is the one sin that cannot be pardoned now or in the life to come.

It is one of the countless reasons why we always need God's Spirit in us and why we must faithfully tell the world about the saving power of Christ to as many as we can before it is too late and we run out of time. I am writing this to myself as well. We may not always sense God's presence, nor should we expect to in this life, but as long as we are in Christ, His Spirit is with us (John 15:5-6, Rom. 8:1-17).

The Return of Christ

So, we have just read that Christ is coming back and that His true followers join the Holy Spirit in desiring His return. But before all that, the book of Revelation, along with many of the books of the New Testament describe a period of Earth's history where there will be unparalleled distress and destruction.

A question in many people's hearts and on many people's lips throughout the many years is - when will all this happen? It was a question the disciples asked Jesus 2,000 years ago, saying: "when will this happen, and what will be the sign of your coming and of the end of the age?" (Matt. 24:3). Jesus responded by giving a long list of prophetic events that will happen, which will all point towards His return to Earth (see: Matt. 24, Mark 13 and Luke 21). Yet, before all that He made this profound seven-word warning: "Watch out that no one deceives you" (Matt. 24:4).

Warnings about being deceived during 'the last days' appear regularly throughout the New Testament - from this point on until the final chapters of Revelation. For instance, Paul states quite boldly that,

> The Spirit <u>clearly</u> says that in later times some will abandon the faith and follow deceiving spirits and things taught by demons... Watch your life and doctrine closely. Persevere in them, because if you do, you will save both yourself and your hearers."

1 Timothy 4;1, 16

It is the Spirit who is making him aware of these things. If you see all of that chapter, you will notice there are clear instructions about keeping safe from deception.

Deception comes from the Devil (Gen. 3:13, John 8:44, Rev. 12:9) and when it spreads it causes disunity, confusion, worry, persecution, a loss of freedom and even a loss of faith. All that will be key prophetic markers of the final years before Christ's return. It is His deep desire that His followers living in any generation, but especially during the last of the last days remain true to Him, His Word and His Spirit. In 2 Corinthians, Paul warns us against false apostles and teachers who would try to lead others astray:

> I am afraid that just as Eve was deceived by the snake's cunning, your minds may somehow be led astray from your sincere and pure devotion to Christ. For if someone comes to you and preaches a Jesus other than the Jesus we preached, <u>or if you receive a different spirit from the Spirit you received</u>, or a different gospel from the one you accepted, you put up with it easily enough.

> 2 Corinthians 14:3-4

What is concerning about that it is the possibility of receiving another spirit other than 'the Holy Spirit' and in conjunction with Paul's words further up about the doctrines of demons multiplying in the last days, it is imperative that we do not become influenced internally or externally by false spirits who will gain power as time goes on.

Individual believers and church bodies who fail to keep a check on their faith and doctrine can allow the Devil and his demons ease of access. As mentioned in the previous chapter, towards the end of His ministry Jesus shared three consecutive Kingdom parables about keeping one's guard and being faithful to the very end (Matt. 25). Each parable is about a righteous group of believers and a falsely righteous group. The first Parable (verses 1-13) is about five foolish bridesmaids and five wise bridesmaids who according to Jewish tradition had to get ready for a torch procession arrival of the bridegroom. He could come at any time of night.

On face value, the wise and the foolish bridesmaids seem the same:

- They all appear to be on time for the event
- They all slept, which the parable does not criticise
- They all brought their lamps and put them in order
- They would have all looked the same for the occasion too

However, the foolish women were not truly prepared, because they did not take any extra oil with them, which caused their lights to go out. That is the only difference between them and the wise bridesmaids. That was the laziness, not the sleeping. Lazy people don't want to do anything extra. They want the joys of life, without going the extra mile. What helps the flame to grow? Oil!

The oil used here would most likely be olive oil, which was used a lot in Biblical times for many uses. In the scriptures, olive oil is used as a symbol of the anointing and the working of God's Spirit in a person's life. It's a sign that you know God, that you belong to Him and that His blessing is on you (Heb. 2:2-4). Without oil, half of the wedding party was not ready for the bridegroom, just as without the leading, guiding and anointing of the Spirit of Christ in our lives, we cannot truly be on fire for God. Jesus said to receive the Holy Spirit (John 20:22), because without the Spirit, our initial flame (if indeed we had one) will go out - for we will try to do things in our own strength.

Paul said:

You, however, are not in the realm of the flesh but are in the realm of the Spirit, if indeed the Spirit of God lives in you. And if anyone does not have the Spirit of Christ, they do not belong to Christ. But if Christ is in you, your body is dead because of sin, yet the Spirit gives you life because of righteousness.

Romans 8:9-10

In line with the humble words of John the Baptist, we must decrease as Christ increases (John 3:30). It is He who lives the Christian life through us. By His Spirit He gives us the strength we need each and every day.

I have been crucified with Christ and I no longer live,
but Christ lives in me. The life I now live in the body, I
live by faith in the Son of God, who loved me and gave
himself for me.

Galatians 2:20

If ever we will see another revival again in this country, it will
be (as always) by the Holy Spirit of God stirring up the hearts of the
faithful and bringing many more to Christ. As with the first
Christian revival 2,000 years ago, when the Spirit of God fell on
those faithful few in the Temple and 3,000 more were added to
their number by the end of the day. We must submit to the true
Spirit of God.

Notice how the New Testament emphasises His holiness - He
is referred to as the *Holy* Spirit almost 100 times, compared to only
three times in the Old Testament. We must surely become more
holy if we are to see real change in our lives, our churches and the
nations. Remember how God required man to turn from his wicked
ways and repent before He changes things on a personal scale and a
larger one too (2 Chron. 7:14, Jer. 18, Jas. 5:16).

I do not believe we live in an age that promotes the concept
of holiness. In fact, the opposite is true. Even in the church, there is
a lack of teaching on it. I would recommend studying it in the Bible
and then acting upon it. I am writing to myself here as well. I would
also suggest reading *The Hole in our Holiness* (2014) by the great
American author Keven De Young.

I do not believe God will bring revival if the church is consistently disobedient to His Word in several areas. He will not revive that which He has not built. If we remove the areas that are unpleasing to Him and replace them with submission to the Word, He can then revive us by the Spirit. In the 16th century, we had a reformation and then revival and revival followed from the 18th century until the 20th, but now we need a new reformation and transformation in order for God's Spirit to move again.

How we discern what is from the Spirit of God and what is not?

The Apostle John tells his readers:

...do not believe every spirit, but test the spirits to see whether they are from God, for many false prophets have gone out into the world.

1 John 4:1

The measures of whether an apostle, a teacher, a prophet, a church or a so-called Christian movement is false or not involves looking at:

- their doctrines - are they in line with scripture or are they adding or taking away from it? Are they always pressurising you for your money by teaching about prosperity all the time?

- their fruit - is what they are doing producing good, loving, holy results in line with scripture?

- their words - how much do they talk about Jesus Christ or apply the words of the Bible?

- their behaviour - are they acting in strange, aggressive, self-promoting ways not consistent with the working of the Holy Spirit?

John continues by saying helping us discern truth from falsity in the spiritual realm:

> This is how you can recognize the Spirit of God: Every spirit that acknowledges that Jesus Christ has come in the flesh is from God, but every spirit that does not acknowledge Jesus is not from God. This is the spirit of the antichrist, which you have heard is coming and even now is already in the world... Who is the liar? It is whoever denies that Jesus is the Christ. Such a person is the antichrist - denying the Father and the Son.

> 1 John 4:2-3 and 2:22

So, a true believer will acknowledge Jesus as the Christ - the Messiah who came in the flesh. They have the Spirit of God in them. I have noticed that there are an increasing number of so-called Christian churches and ministries who are actually denying either the humanity or divinity of Christ in some way. Namely the latter. They also make God out to be weak and almost dependant on us - as though were god.

I saw a video of a man preaching at a very popular 'church' in America, saying that Jesus appeared to him in a dream asking him for forgiveness! Jesus - the sinless Saviour of the world. Another leader at that same 'church' said that the Holy Spirit was like the "genie in the bottle from Aladdin" who was "sneaky", "silly" and blue in colour. Such words are heretically and may even be blasphemous.

Along with an increasingly number of so-called Christian groups are teaching dangerous doctrines, particularly in the areas of the supernatural, the Holy Spirit and on healing. They obsess about them, teaching that we should have a virtually perfect life day to day with no illnesses and no problems and that we can command them to all go and therefore control our destiny. Sometimes God leaves us with illnesses and problems and other times we are set free from them. God never promises a perfect, care-free life.

Paul had constant trials throughout his life and even had a "thorn in the flesh" (2 Cor.11:16-33; 12:7-9). To Timothy, Paul said that a little wine would help him with his frequent illnesses (1 Tim. 5:23). Peter says we do go through fiery trials, persecutions and physical afflictions which only serve to strengthen us so long as we persevere in faith in the face of them (see: 1 Pet. 4-5).

A lot of Charismatic churches promote unusual forms of worship, which result in the leaders and many in the congregation showing strange behaviours, such as excessive shaking, convulsing, screaming, and even people acting like animals and running around as though they are on fire. They say it's the Holy Spirit, but surely such manifestations might actually remind one of the disturbed people Jesus and the early disciples encountered in their ministries. Those people needed the Holy Spirit and so do many people today. Indeed, there are many who are receiving "a different spirit", by being taught "a different Gospel "about "a different Jesus" from the real one. The deception is very cunning. We must not be fooled by it or afraid to challenge it.

Such people who justify the above behaviours often state that who are we to restrict the Holy Spirit? Yet, Paul sets out boundaries for church services so as to retain peace and order and to reduce confusion and disorder (1 Cor. 11-15). God also established the proper ways to worship and honour Him in the first four Commandments (Exod. 20:1-11).

Many wacky, over the top Charismatics sometimes speak of being "drunk in the Holy Spirit" to explain their erratic behaviour during worship services. I've heard that phrase too many times over the years. Such a statement is surely insulting to God. The proponents of it justify it by saying the early disciples were "drunk in the Holy Spirit" at Pentecost. Yet if you look at the relevant passage, it was unbelievers who referred to the disciples being drunk. Peter rebukes them saying they are "not drunk", but rather have received the promised Holy Spirit (Acts 2:13-17). Paul states in Ephesians 5:18 to "not get drunk with wine, for that is debauchery, but be filled with the Spirit".

So, as we can see, there are members of churches and ministries who are following questionable doctrines about the Spirit and are experiencing weird supernatural manifestations which are actually not from the Spirit at all. I have not named such groups as I do not think this is the place to do that, but I would encourage you to keep your guard and if you feel you may have received something false in you, then seek the Lord and ask Him to guide you to a person or a group who understand these things and can pray over you for healing and deliverance.

I strongly believe we are facing increasingly dark and dangerous times. The scriptures confirm this, yet God is still with us and His power does not wax or wain. He is unlimited. There will be major temptations to deny Christ so as to avoid persecution and even death. We must remain in Christ and He will remain in us (John 15:5-6).

Maybe you are battling against temptations or you feel you may be being deceived or perhaps you are being oppressed by demonic or generational ties or maybe you are being used or abused by a family member, a so-called friend or your church leadership. Ask God now to help you. He'll hear you through all the deceptive, accusative words of the enemy and his demons. God is immeasurably greater and more powerful than the world, the flesh and the Devil.

Be honest with God, even if you're sure that you're being genuine before Him. Perhaps you feel your prayers are selfish. Just confess all to Him, including sins you may not realise you committed or that you've forgotten about. His Holy Spirit will guide you into all truth and healing. You will overcome all these things through being faithful to the Word which has the power to save, heal and believer you; by the blood of the Lamb shed for you so you can be forgiven and by loving God more than anything else in your life (see: Revelation 12:11).

Who then is the one who condemns? No one. Christ Jesus who died—more than that, who was raised to life - is at the right hand of God and is also interceding for us. Who shall separate us from the love of Christ? Shall trouble or hardship or persecution or famine or nakedness or danger or sword? As it is written:

"For your sake we face death all day long; we are considered as sheep to be slaughtered."

No, in all these things we are more than conquerors through him who loved us. For I am convinced that neither death nor life, neither angels nor demons, neither the present nor the future, nor any powers, neither height nor depth, nor anything else in all creation, will be able to separate us from the love of God that is in Christ Jesus our Lord.

Romans 8:36-39,
see also Psalm 44:22

Notice that Paul does not include 'us' in that long list of things that cannot separate us from God. So, the only one who can separate you from the love of God is you! But if you come near to God, He will come to you (see: Jas. 4:8 and also 2 Tim. 2). He is faithful to you even when we are unfaithful to Him. It is His Holy, mighty, amazing Spirit who draws all of us back to our Heavenly Father and to our Saviour Jesus Christ - if we let Him.

Let us "keep in step with the Spirit" (Gal. 5:25) by resisting the fleshly, worldly desires and join "the Spirit and the bride [in saying] 'Come!'...let the one who hears say, 'Come!' Let the one who is thirsty come; and let the one who wishes take the free gift of the water of life." The 'water of life' or the 'living water' refers to the Holy Spirit. He comes freely, as a gentle, refreshing, restoring, healing power with absolutely no price tag attached. Just come as you are. All we must do is receive Him through faith and repentance.

What does Jesus say back to us: **"Yes, I am coming soon."** and we say **"Amen. Come, Lord Jesus."** (Revelation 22:17, 20).

~

All who are thirsty,
All who are weak,
Just come to the fountain,
Dip your heart in the stream of life.
Let the pain and the sorrow
Be washed away.
In the waves of His mercy,
As the deep cries out to deep, we sing...

Come, Lord Jesus come,
Come, Lord Jesus come,
Come, Lord Jesus come,
Come, Lord Jesus come!

Holy Spirit, come,
Holy Spirit, come,
Holy Spirit, come,
Holy Spirit, come!

Come and breathe on us again,
Come and breathe on us again,
Come and visit us again,
Come and visit us again!

~

Worship Songs to the Spirit

Here is a list of recommended hymns, praise and worship songs about the Holy Spirit. You may not like them all or even the churches where they originated from, but I believe they all have powerful truths about the Spirit of God which honour Him and draw the believer closer to God:

All who are Thirsty - Glenn Robertson, Brenton Brown
Breathe on Me Breath of God - Edwin Hatch, Robert Jackson
Breathe on Me - Darlene Zschech
Holy Spirit Come and Fill this Place - CeCe Winans
Come Lord Jesus (Great is the Darkness) - Noel Richards
Consuming Fire - Tim Hughes
Glorify Thy Name (Father, we Love You) - Donna Adkins
Holy! Holy! Holy! Lord God Almighty
Holy Spirit, Living Breath of God - Keith Getty, Stuart Townend
Holy Spirit, Rain Down - Darlene Zschech
Holy Spirit, Thou Art Welcome - Dottie Rambo, David Huntsinger
How Great Is Our God - Chris Tomlin
Not by Might - Robin Mark
Spirit of the Living God - Daniel Iverson
Spirit of the Living God - Paul Armstrong
Sweet Holy Spirit - The Isaacs
The Lord Is My Salvation - Keith and Kristyn Getty
The Potter's Hand - Darlene Zschech
There is a Redeemer - Keith Green
Welcome in this Place - Miriam Webster

Sadly, there are 'Christian' songs out there which appear spiritual, but are more about the experience of worship, rather than the focus of the worship - which should always be God. They appeal to the congregation's soul more so than their spirit. Since the turn of this century, I have noticed how many worship songs are sounding more ethereal, overly-repetitive and New Agey. The worship leaders tend to get carried away and the attention falls off God and onto themselves. I've seen some strange manifestations occur in people as a result of singing those songs over and over again. Some people even become catatonic or start shaking uncontrollably. That is not meant to be a judgment, but rather an observation and a shared concern.

I would strongly urge you to ask God to give you discernment on these things and if you look up some of the songs above to listen to online. I would also be cautious as to who is singing them.

I ask that I am not led astray by any sort of false worship, and that I do not incorrectly and unfairly discount certain worship songs and worship leaders. Sometimes I pick up a bad sense from a leader or a team who are leading worship. There is something not quite right in my spirit when I see them lead worship or hear the song being played. Certain songs feel wrong too even if the lyrics appear to be Biblical.

It can be that what goes on in that church and what has (shall we say) been poured into their songs is not of the Holy Spirit.

Of course, we don't want to incorrectly accuse anyone of operating with the enemy as some around Jesus accused Him of once, but we have go back to the Word and be led by His Spirit to discern what spirits are at work (1 Cor. 12:10). We must see the fruit being produced and test every spirit to see if they are from God (1 John 4:1-5).

List of Trinitarian Scriptures

Many of the below passages refer to just two persons of the Godhead, however almost all refer to three. Despite many recent attacks on the doctrine of the Trinity, the scriptures are full of passages which clearly show all three unique persons as equally divine.

Genesis 1:1-2, 26; 3:22; 6:3; 11:6-7; 18-19:22
Psalm 2; 139:7-10
Proverbs 30:3-6
Isaiah 6:8; 9:6-7; 42:1; 48:16-17; 52:13-53:12
Ezekiel 2:2; 3:12, 14; 36:27
Daniel 7:13-14
Joel 2:28-29
Micah 5:1-3
Matthew 1:23; 3:16-17; 12:18 (quote of Isa. 42:1); 22:41-45; 28:19
Luke 1:34-35; 3:21-23; 11:13, 21-22; 24:49
John 1:1-18; 3:5-8, 16, 34-36; 10:27-36; 14:14-17, 26; 15:26; 16:3-17:26; 20:21-22
Acts 1:7-8; 2:32-33, 38-29; 5:1-11, 29-32, 7:55-56, 29-32; 10:38; 15:7-12; 19:1-8, 20:20-24
Romans 1:1-4; 8; 14:17-18; 15:15-19, 30
1 Corinthians 6:11; 8:6; 12:4-6
2 Corinthians 3:17; 13:14
Galatians 4:4-7; 6:1-10
Colossians 1:15-17; 2:8-10; 3:16-17
Philippians 1:19, 27-29; 2:1-11; 3:3
Ephesians 1:17; 2:13-22; 3:16-17; 4:4-6; 5:18-20
1 Thessalonians 1:1-10; 3:11-13; 5:16-28
2 Thessalonians 2:13-17
Titus 3:4-7
Hebrews 2:3-4; 3:7-15; 6:1-6; 9:14; 10:5-16, 26-31
1 Peter 1:1-2
1 John 2:22-24; 4:13-16; 5:7-8
Jude 1:20-21
Revelation 1:1-11; 3:5-6, 21-22; 4-5; 20:10; 22:16-18

The three major writing prophets of the Bible are Jeremiah, Isaiah and Ezekiel. Their books are placed near each other in the Biblical canon and what is amazing is that:

- Jeremiah reveals to us God as the Father
- Isaiah reveals to us God as the Son
- Ezekiel reveals to us God as the Spirit

In the prayer that Jesus taught us - the 'Our Father', there are six petitions. The first three are about what God wants from us and the second three are about what we need from God. In both sets of petitions, one can see the role of the three persons of the Trinity:

PART / PETITION	THE PRAYER	THE TRINITY
Introduction and Invocation	'Our Father in heaven,	The Father
1st petition	hallowed be your name,	It is the Father's name that is being honoured.
2nd petition	your kingdom come,	The Father's Kingdom came through Jesus His Son's first coming and will be fully come when He returns.
3rd petition	your will be done,	We can only do the Father's will by the Spirit.
Mid-Conclusion	on earth as it is in heaven.	-

4th petition	Give us today our daily bread.	Jesus said the Father feeds both man and animals and gives all we need.
5th petition	And forgive us our debts, as we also have forgiven our debtors.	Only through the death of the Father's Son on the cross can we have forgiveness of our sins. We forgive because God in Christ forgave us.
6th petition	And lead us not into temptation, but deliver us from the evil one.'	The Spirit of the Father helps us in our weaknesses and trials by leading us and speaking through us.
Conclusion and Doxology	for yours is the kingdom and the power and the glory forever. Amen	The Father

If you want to know more about the Holy Spirit and know Him more personally, there are also five books of the New Testament which speak of Him more than any others and they are all placed together: Luke, John, Acts, Romans and 1 Corinthians.

It is then in the next book along that we read the famous prayer of grace often said at the end of church services across the world. It is a personal prayer I want to share with you as my hope for more truth and unity amongst the body of believers to which we all belong:

May the grace of <u>the Lord Jesus Christ</u>, and the love of <u>God</u>, and the fellowship of <u>the Holy Spirit</u> be with you all. Amen.

2 Corinthians 13:14

We also read this prayer too:

Now all of us can come to <u>the Father</u> through <u>the same Holy Spirit</u> because of what <u>Christ</u> has done for us.

Ephesians 2:18

And look at the Trinitarian nature of his preaching and Christian walk before all people he encountered:

I have declared to both Jews and Greeks that they must turn to <u>God</u> in repentance and have faith in our <u>Lord Jesus</u>. "And now, compelled by <u>the Spirit</u>, I am going to Jerusalem, not knowing what will happen to me there. I only know that in every city <u>the Holy Spirit</u> warns me that prison and hardships are facing me. However, I consider my life worth nothing to me; my only aim is to finish the race and complete the task <u>the Lord Jesus</u> has given me—the task of testifying to the good news of <u>God</u>'s grace.

Acts 20:20-24

Notice the '<u>Father</u> / <u>Son</u> / <u>Spirit</u>', then
       '<u>Spirit</u> / <u>Son</u> / <u>Father</u>' pattern there.

How do I become a Christian?

If you begin to feel as though you need to come into relationship with God, there are these helpful steps that you need to take in order for that to happen. This is the beginning of what is called 'repentance'. Along with faith, it is a gift of God that needs to be found in our thoughts, our words and our deeds.

1. **Repent to God the Father in order for Him to forgive you:**

   - <u>in thought</u> - by changing your mind and heart about your life and realising that it needs to change from being a sinful life to a spiritual life.

   - <u>in word</u> - by confessing the sins of your life to God and asking Him to forgive you of them. You won't possibly be able to remember everything you've done wrong, but God does and He will wash those sins away as though they had never happened. He changes your past! You may suffer from some of the mistakes you have made, but He will give you strength to deal with them. They no longer have to haunt you. See: 1 John 1:8-9.

   - <u>in deed</u> - by taking practical steps to live a life than moves away from sin. Righting the wrongs that you can. Repentance means to turn the other way, once you have changed your mind towards God and realise your need for Him (Matthew 3:8, Acts 26:20).

2. Believe in God the Son to save you:

- <u>in thought</u> - by believing in your mind and heart that Jesus died in your place to make you free your sins and so that you could have the forgiveness from the Father. Believe also that God raised Him from the dead to give you everlasting life with Him (Romans 10:9-10).

- <u>in word</u> - by confessing with your mouth 'Jesus is Lord', so that you are saying He is now in charge of your life and not yourself. When a couple get married they hopefully do so out of a deep love each other from their hearts. They trust each other and therefore, verbally state before God and man that they will commit themselves to each other. Every person that Jesus called to believe in Him, He called publicly. Even if you make this commitment in private, speak out that you believe He is Lord. He hears your ever word (Romans 10:9-10).

- <u>in deed</u> - by reading His Word, the Bible. The Gospel of Mark is a good place to begin. It tells us the life of Jesus in a straightforward, action-packed way that is best for new believers. Look at these scriptures also: Psalm 139, Romans 8, 10, 1 John 1:8-9 and Ephesians 2:1-10.

3. Receive God the Spirit to guide you:

- <u>in thought</u> - by inviting God to live within you, as you become the Temple of His Spirit (1 Corinthians 6:19-20).
- <u>in word</u> - by acknowledging reception of His Spirit and asking God to show you how to pray in the Spirit
- <u>in deed</u> - find a Spirit-filled church that believe sin the gifts of the Spirit and ask someone one to pray over you if you feel you need more of the Spirit (Acts 19:1-7, Ephesians 5:18-19).

4. Take other important practical steps of faith:

- Pray every day - and base your prayers on the *Our Father* prayer that Jesus taught - putting God's wants before your needs. The prayer is meant to be a daily one and is found in the sixth chapter of Matthew's Gospel and in the eleventh chapter of Luke's Gospel.
- Confess your sins every day - to keep short accounts with God. The petition about being forgiven and forgiving others is found in the *Our Father* prayer.
- Read and study the scriptures everyday - perhaps start with the New Testament, so that you read about Jesus first and how he fulfilled the laws and prophecies of the Old Testament. Then study the Old Testament.
- Worship God every day - sing spiritual songs to Him of thanks and praise! Get to know the great Christian hymns and worship songs.
- Ask God to help you find a good, Bible-believing, Spirit-led church that honours Him - The book of Hebrews in the New

Testament tells us not to neglect the body of believers. The Book of Acts records how the early church met regularly to worship God, to build each other up, to share fellowship and communion, to hear and teach the Word of God and to pray together as one. Jesus said that even if just two or three gathered in His name, He would be with them in their midst. He never leaves or forsakes us, but we must also remain Him forever.

- get baptised in the name of the Father, the Son and the Spirit - this can be done after you've found a good church and have got to know the leaders there and feel confident and ready to ask them to be baptised. They should guide you in the process.

- Go and spread the Good News that you now believe! - this was Christ's command to all believers. Don't keep what you now know - tell the world about Jesus. His Spirit will give you the words to say to you trust in Him.

In doing all these things you will be born-again; your life will increasingly resemble the Lord Jesus Christ's life, as you are led step by step by His Spirit, who'll eventually bring back to your heavenly Father so that you will be perfect, just as He is! Never look back or turn away from this wonderful walk! It will be very heard at times, but Jesus promised to never leave us, so long as we stay with Him!

God bless you on your journey of faith!

REFERENCES

Armstrong, Paul. (1984). *Spirit of the Living God*. Restoration Music, Ltd. (Admin. by Crossroad Distributors Pty. Ltd.).

Brown, Brenton; Robertson, Glenn. (1998). Vineyard Songs (UK/Eire). All rights reserved. International copyright secured.

Buscaglia, Leo. *Leo Buscaglia Quotes* [online]. Available at: http://www.brainyquote.com/quotes/quotes/l/leobuscagl150305.html (Accessed: 13 October 2016).

Creeds and authorized affirmations of faith [online]. Available at: https://www.churchofengland.org/prayer-worship/worship/texts/newpatterns/contents/sectione.aspx (Accessed: 14 October 2016).

Dawkins, Richard. (2006). *The God Delusion*, p.33. Bantam.

De Young, Kevin. (2014). *The Hole in our Holiness*, Crossway.

Ellicott, C. J. (1897). *A New Testament commentary for English readers*. 2 Peter. London, Cassell and Co.

Graham, Billy. (1978). *The Holy Spirit*, p. 148. Thomas Nelson, Nashville. 1988 edition.

ibid. pp.159-160.

Kilby, Clyde S. (1976). *Tolkien and The Silmarillion*, p. 59. Wheaton, Ill.: Harold Shaw.

Miller, Paul. (2011). *Following* [online - audio]. Available at: http://mp3.dukest.org/2011_09_25_PM_web.mp3 (Accessed: 13 October 2016).

Miller, Paul (2014). *The Bible* [online - audio]. Available at: http://mp3.dukest.org/2014_03_30_PM_web.mp3 (Accessed: 18 October 2016).

Miller, Paul (2015) *quoted from: Paul Miller.* (2015) [YouTube video], added by Sam Miller [online - video]. Available at: https://youtu.be/Tj11WSnHYUY (Accessed: 29 September 2016).

Newton, John. (1779) *Amazing Grace*, 'Dictionary of American Hymnology'. Available at: http://www.hymnary.org/text/amazing_grace_how_sweet_the_s ound (Accessed on 19 August 2016).

Pawson, David. (1999). *Unlocking the Bible*, pp. 884-885, London, HarperCollinsPublishers, (2007 edition).

- The example of using all nine fruits of the Spirit in one situation was adapted from David's Pawson's book *Word and Spirit Together: Uniting Charismatics and Evangelicals.* Pawson, David. *Word and Spirit Together Pt 2 by David Pawson,* added in 2009 by David PawsonNZ [online]. Available at: https://www.youtube.com/watch?v=aFCPwjNdxVA (Accessed: 31 August 2016).

- *David Pawson - Charismatics and Evangelicals* (2016). YouTube, added by 'General Han Solo' [online]. Available at: https://www.youtube.com/watch?v=GSA-AfHJJq4 (Accessed: 27 September 2016).

The Wizard of Oz (1939). Directed by Victor Fleming [film]. New York, distributed by Loews Inc.

Tuttle, Robert G. Jr. *John Wesley and the Gifts of the Holy Spirit* [online]. Available at: http://ucmpage.org/articles/rtuttle1.html (Accessed: 12 October 2016).

Tolkien, J.R.R (1954a). *The Fellowship of the Ring*, pp. 433-434, HarperCollinsPublishers, Hammersmith, London, Film tie-in edition, 2001.

Tolkien, J.R.R. (1954b). *The Two Towers*, pp. 113-114, HarperCollinsPublishers, Hammersmith, London, Film tie-in edition, 2001.

Watson, David. *The Word of God. Quotations to stir heart and mind.* Available at: http://www.christianitytoday.com/ct/2001/october22/23.40.html (Accessed: 13 October 2016).

Wigglesworth, Smith. (1947). *Two Distinct Moves.* Available at: http://www.worldprayer.org.uk/images/PDF/Wigglesworth-Darnell-prophecies.pdf (Accessed: 13 October 2016).

Wikipedia (2016). *Filioque* [online], 5 October 2016. Available at: https://en.wikipedia.org/wiki/Filioque (Accessed: 14 October 2016)

Wikipedia (2016). *Quakers* [online], 14 October 2016. Available at: https://en.wikipedia.org/wiki/Quakers (Accessed: 14 October 2016)

Wikipedia (2016). *Secret Fire* [online], Available at: http://lotr.wikia.com/wiki/Secret_Fire (9 September 2016) Clink on relevant links (i.e. Valinor (for Anor) and Udûn) within the document for more info.

Wikipedia (2016). *Saint Patrick's Breastplate* [online]. Available at: https://en.wikipedia.org/wiki/Saint_Patrick%27s_Breastplate (Accessed: 14 October 2016).

Wikipedia (2016). *William Wilberforce* [online]. Available at: https://en.wikipedia.org/wiki/William_Wilberforce (Accessed: 14 October 2016).

Wurmbrand, Richard. (1988). *Alone With God: New Sermons from Solitary Confinement*, p. 25, Hodder and Stoughton, London.

- See also: *Richard and Sabina Wurmbrand Interview in 1989* (2014), YouTube, added by 'Promotions' [online]. Available at: https://www.youtube.com/watch?v=helKvd5ymeE (Accessed: 29 September 2016).

Printed in Great Britain
by Amazon

63655744R00139